UNOFFICIAL
DOCTOR
WHO
THE BIG BOOK OF
LISTS

UNOFFICIAL
DOCTOR
WHO
THE BIG BOOK OF
LISTS

Cameron K. McEwan
Illustrated by Andrew Skilleter

Race Point
PUBLISHING

RACE POINT PUBLISHING
An imprint of Quarto Publishing Group USA Inc.
276 Fifth Avenue, Suite 205
New York, NY 10001

RACE POINT PUBLISHING and the distinctive Race Point Publishing logo are trademarks of Quarto Publishing Group USA Inc.

ISBN 978 1 63106 012-7

Library of Congress Cataloging-in-Publication Data is available

Cover Art and all interior illustrations © by Andrew Skilleter

Interior Design by Guido Caroti

Printed in China

10 9 8 7 6 5 4 3 2 1

Contents

Introduction 7

Characters & Companions 9

Production 33

By the Numbers 73

Pop Culture 91

Story Lines 139

The Doctor & His Toys 199

Quiz Time! 239

Quiz Time! Answers 249

About the Author 252

About the Illustrator 254

Photo credit: Sebastian J.Brook

In 2014, my first book, *The Who's Who of Doctor Who*, was published—and what a moment that was! I can't tell you what a thrill it was seeing it in bookstores around the world. It was both surreal and hugely exciting.

One of the highlights from the publishing of the book was bumping into a Mr. Peter Capaldi and showing him the cover of the book, in which he takes pride of place. Peter was visibly taken aback as this was the first *Doctor Who* book to feature him on the cover. His fanboy glee was more than evident.

The Who's Who of Doctor Who also introduced me to legendary artist Andrew Skilleter, who is so familiar to those who grew up buying the TARGET novelizations and *Doctor Who* on VHS. He was kind enough to supply the amazing artwork in that book and you can see more of his astounding creations throughout this book, too. It was a joy working with Andrew and wonderful to see his take on modern *Doctor Who*.

Like 2013, the 50th anniversary year, 2014 also proved to be an eventful time in the world of *Who*. I've been lucky enough to attend some big events including the world premiere of "Deep Breath," the first full Peter Capaldi episode as the Doctor. I was also invited onto the set of the Series 8 finale ("Dark Water"/"Death In Heaven"), where I stood just meters from Capaldi and Michelle Gomez (who plays Missy) as they filmed taking selfies with Cybermen outside St. Paul's Cathedral on a warm summer's day. This was an unforgettable moment, and my thanks to Edward Russell for the invitation.

Even better was taking a trip to Roath Lock studios in Cardiff, Wales, the home of *Doctor Who*, to watch the filming of the 2014 Christmas special. After a lovely interview with Santa and his elves (Nick Frost and co.), I was treated to a look round the TARDIS (and, boy, did I have a good look at those bookshelves—the Doctor has numerous copies of the Bible in there, fact fans!) and then had a sneak peek at filming itself, which involved those horrible Dream Crabs! *shivers*

As soon as the first book was released, my publisher was keen for a second installment, and we agreed on this, a list book. Those familiar with *Blogtor Who* will know that over the years I have amassed a number of lists for the site (some of which have been reappropriated and updated here). I like to think that they're a bit different to the more mundane lists you'll find elsewhere and have a certain amount of fun and personality about them.

Of course, underlying each list are cold hard facts. Facts from over fifty years of storytelling. Facts that, sometimes (just sometimes), contradict previous facts. And sometimes, *future* facts. And often at the same time. But isn't that the nature of *Doctor Who*? Anyway, I do hope you enjoy these lists and the beautiful accompanying art from Andrew. We had such a fun time putting it all together!

Finally, thanks to everyone who has contacted me, either online or in person. Over the past few years or so, it's been wonderful attending conventions and events and speaking to fans and to those who have liked my work. I'm always very touched and very grateful when it happens.

Cameron K. McEwan

(aka The Blogtor)

CHARACTERS & COMPANIONS

CHARACTERS & COMPANIONS

A Dozen Doses of the Queen of England

In the UK, the only thing people love more than *Doctor Who* is the Queen. Well, not quite, but Her Majesty has had an interesting relationship with the show, and fact fans may note that in real life she is an actual *Doctor Who* fan! Here are the moments in *Who* history that have involved Elizabeth II.

12. "Inferno" (1970)

Not a happy one to kick off with, but the fascist regime of the parallel UK executed the Royal Family in 1943, when poor Liz was just seventeen years old. Blimey.

11. "Turn Left" (2008)

Likewise, in this Tenth Doctor alternate universe story, the Royal Family was killed when the intergalactic cruise ship Titanic crashed into Buckingham Palace one fateful Christmas Day. Thankfully Donna Noble saved the day.

10. "Mawdryn Undead" (1983)

This excellent Fifth Doctor story hopped between the Queen's Silver Jubilee in 1977 and contemporary Britain. You'll see lots of bunting, tight tees, and the Doctor revealing his Queen knowledge by knowing the Jubilee date precisely. He must like her.

9. "Tooth & Claw" (2006)

Rose asks the Doctor, "So the Royal Family are werewolves?" after he suggests that the blood sport–lovin' nature of the Royal DNA may raise its head in the early twenty-first century. Not our Queen, surely…?

8. "Robot" (1974)

The Fourth Doctor received an invitation to dine at the Palace after his heroics with a giant robot, though it was left to the Brigadier to decline.

7. "The End of Time" (2010)

Here we almost get an appearance by Her Majesty as Wilf Mott sits down respectfully to watch the Queen's Speech on television (a Christmas Day tradition in the UK). Though as soon as the words "The Queen" appear, a rather mysterious woman materializes and has a chat with Donna Noble's grandfather. Of course, Elizabeth would later find her head replaced by that of the Master for a short while.

6. **"The Beast Below" (2010)**

Liz Ten reveals that the Doctor had "tea and scones" with, using the future vernacular, Liz Two. Judging by his previous encounters with royalty, that could be a euphemism.

5. **"The Christmas Invasion" (2005)**

"It's hardly the Queen's Speech, I'm afraid that's been canceled. Did we ask about the Royal Family? Oh, they're on the roof." —Harriet Jones, Prime Minister

4. **"Planet of the Dead" (2009)**

This Easter special reveals a great deal about the relationship between the Time Lord and the Queen. Upon UNIT's return of his TARDIS from the grounds of Buckingham Palace, the Tenth Doctor beams, "Oh, she doesn't mind!"

3. **"The Idiot's Lantern" (2006)**

According to one of the ladies watching the 1953 coronation: "Makes you forget all your troubles." The Doctor's ironic utterance of "God save the Queen, eh?" was intriguing, however. Still, a glimpse of Lizzy, albeit on a battered old black-and-white television.

2. **"Silver Nemesis" (1988)**

An actual, factual sighting! This time, Lizzy takes the dogs for a walk around Windsor Castle while the Seventh Doctor and companion Ace goof around the grounds and spot her. Though the Gallifreyan does take a little while to place her face.

1. **"Voyage of the Damned" (2007)**

Not just an appearance, but the Queen gets some dialogue in this Christmas special. After salutations from Wilf ("Gawd bless her!" he proudly claims) and a mention by the Tenth Doctor ("Her Majesty has got it right, as far as I know"), we see her wave to the starliner Titanic after a near miss with Buckingham Palace. Knowing her savior, Liz Two coos, "Thank you, Doctor. Thank you. Happy Christmas!" Aw, bless.

Funny Quotes

Doctor Who can be quite a serious business, but the Doctor and his chums do like to lighten the atmosphere from time to time. Featured here are some of the more hilarious nuggets delivered over the years.

"You know, you're a classic example of the inverse ratio between the size of the mouth and the size of the brain." —The Fourth Doctor, "The Robots of Death" (1977)

"Lots of planets have a north!" —The Ninth Doctor, "Rose" (2005)

"You fought her off with a water pistol! I bloody love you!" —Donna Noble, "The Fires of Pompeii" (2008)

"Hermits United. We meet up every ten years. Swap stories about caves. It's good fun. For a hermit." —The Tenth Doctor, "Utopia" (2007)

"Good evening. I'm a Lizard Woman from the Dawn of Time, and this is my wife." —Madame Vastra, "The Snowmen" (2012)

"Call yourself a Time Lord? A broken clock keeps better time than you do. At least it's accurate twice a day, which is more than you ever are." —Tegan Jovanka, "The Visitation (1982)

"Do what I do. Hold tight and pretend it's a plan!" —The Eleventh Doctor, "The Doctor, the Widow and the Wardrobe" (2011)

"Nine hundred years of time and space, and I've never been slapped by someone's mother." —The Ninth Doctor, "Aliens of London" (2005)

"Never ignore coincidence. Unless, of course, you're busy. In which case, always ignore coincidence." —The Eleventh Doctor, "The Pandorica Opens" (2010)

"Who looks at a screwdriver and thinks, 'Ooo, this could be a little more sonic?' " —Captain Jack Harkness, "The Doctor Dances" (2005)

"An apple a day keeps the, er… No, never mind." —The Fifth Doctor, "Kinda" (1982)

"Always take a banana to a party, Rose! Bananas are good!" —The Tenth Doctor, "The Girl in the Fireplace" (2006)

"Biting's excellent. It's like kissing, only there's a winner." —Idris, "The Doctor's Wife" (2011)

Funny Things the Daleks Say

3

For a race that doesn't have any emotion, the Daleks sure are a chatty bunch. And how they do like to drop the odd hilarious line. Check out some of their more gigglesome and downright odd lines.

"Embark! Embark! Embark! Embark!" —"The Chase" (1965)

"We can also supply unlimited quantities of fresh vegetables which are forced in artificial sunlight." —"The Daleks" (1963)

"The weight of your body has fallen by seventeen ounces."
—"The Evil of the Daleks" (1967)

"The waste bucket in shaft nine is being lowered now."
—"The Dalek Invasion of Earth" (1964)

"We understand the human mind."
—"The Power of the Daleks" (1966)

"Destroy and rejoice!" —"The Chase" (1965)

"Dizzy Daleks!" —"The Evil of the Daleks" (1967)

"Am exterminated! Am exterminated! Arrrggggh!"
—"The Chase" (1965)

"Explanations are irrelevant. Production targets must be maintained. Inefficient workers slow down production."
—"Day of the Daleks" (1972)

"My vision is impaired. I cannot see."
—"Resurrection of the Daleks" (1984)

"Yes, we know who you are!"
—"Journey's End" (2008)

"Small human female sighted."
—"Remembrance of the Daleks" (1988)

"Totally immobilized."
—"The Chase" (1965)

Another Girl, Another Planet

Along the way, the Doctor has picked up a number of traveling companions in the TARDIS, the majority being from Earth (past, present, and future). They've all been human in form, but there are a select few who joined Team TARDIS who are not from our lovely planet. This is their list. (Apologies to both Kamelion and K9, who are robots, not human.)

Susan

I think we can assume that though we first met her on Earth in "An Unearthly Child" (1963), the Doctor's granddaughter hailed from Gallifrey as we see her leave there with the First Doctor in "The Name of the Doctor" (2013). As an exiled wanderer in the fourth dimension, Susan actually ended up back on Earth when her grandfather left her there in "The Dalek Invasion of Earth" (1964).

Leela

Though very human in form, and another exile, Leela was not from Earth. Never named, her planet is visited by the Fourth Doctor in "The Face of Evil" (1977), where he bumps into the female warrior, ostracized from her tribe, the Sevateem. Her human appearance is explained by the fact that her people were descendants from an Earth colony ship that crashed there many years previous (Sevateem being derived from the original phrase "survey team"). Behind the scenes, Tom Baker and Louise Jameson didn't get on too well, but they have now patched things up and work together on a series of *Doctor Who* audio stories.

Romana

Depending on whether you call her Fred, like the Fourth Doctor wanted to, or Romanadvoratnelundar, her full name, this Time Lady was most definitely a Gallifreyan. Oddly, she only visited Earth twice on her televised adventures—Paris and Brighton—and left her fellow Time Lord to help the Tharils in E-Space (as witnessed in 1981's "Warrior's Gate").

Adric

When the Fourth Doctor and Romana found themselves in E-Space, they planted down on the planet Alzarius, where they came upon math wizard Adric (in 1980's "Full Circle"). He joined the TARDIS crew, but, like the aforementioned Susan, he ended up on Earth. Sadly, the

Alzarian literally ended up on Earth, having crashed smack bang into it (and dying in the process).

Nyssa

Not long after the Fourth Doctor picked up Adric, he also welcomed Nyssa, the young girl from Traken, on board. Though she first met the Time Lord in "The Keeper of Traken" (1981), it wasn't until the following story, "Logopolis" (and Tom Baker's last as the Gallifreyan), when she joined the TARDIS as a regular. Her home, Traken, was destroyed due to some unpleasantness by the Master, meaning Nyssa was never able to return to her birthplace.

Turlough

Or, to give him his full name: Junior Ensign Commander Vislor Turlough. This ginger-haired lad seemed as though he was from Earth, being a pupil at a UK school, but we soon learned in his first story, 1983's "Mawdryn Undead," that he was not human. But it wasn't until his final story with the Doctor, 1984's "Planet of Fire," that we found out his home world was Trion, where he returned upon discovering his political prisoner status had been rescinded.

Excuse Me, Did You Drop Something?

The Doctor can be quite a modest and humble man at times, while at other times, he does like to boast about the amazing people he has befriended in his travels in space and time. Here is a collection of his biggest name-drops of famous Earthlings.

Cleopatra

Mickey Smith revealed that the Tenth Doctor had mentioned the Egyptian Queen in passing, even referring to her as "Cleo," denoting a certain familiarity (2006's "The Girl in the Fireplace"). The Fourth Doctor noted in "The Masque of Mandragora" (1976), "You know, the finest swordsman I ever saw was a captain in Cleopatra's bodyguard."

Stevie Wonder

The Doctor's on-off girlfriend/wife River Song told her father, Rory, in "A Good Man Goes to War" (2011) that she had a date with the Time Lord in 1814, where soul legend Stevie Wonder sang to her under London Bridge.

Houdini

In "Planet of the Spiders" (1974), the Third Doctor used a "little trick" he'd learned from Harry Houdini—compressing his muscles to escape a web. Just a few episodes later, in "Revenge of the Cybermen" (1975), the Fourth Doctor claimed, "I used to untangle Turk's Head eye-splice with the grommets I picked up from Houdini." Fact fans will note that the escapologist gets a name-check in 2008's "Planet of the Ood" (by Donna) and 2010's "The Vampires of Venice."

Freud

In the 1996 TV Movie, the Eighth Doctor told Grace that he met the founding father of psychoanalysis. Immediately after, the Time Lord revealed that he also met…

Marie Curie

And knew her "intimately," no less!

Frank Sinatra

"A Christmas Carol" (2010) saw the Eleventh Doctor show off a picture of himself with Father Christmas at the singer's "hunting lodge" in 1953.

Beethoven

After displaying his musical skills in "The Lazarus Experiment" (2007), the Tenth Doctor told companion Martha that "if you hang around with Beethoven, you're bound to pick a few things up."

Benjamin Franklin

So familiar with "The First American" was the Time Lord that he referred to the polymath as "my mate Ben" in "Smith and Jones" (2007). The Tenth Doctor went on to reveal that he was present during Franklin's investigations into electricity and lightning: "That was a day and a half. I got rope burns off that kite, and then I got soaked."

Janis Joplin

The Tenth Doctor stated in 2007's "Gridlock" that he got his coat from the 1960s singer.

Christopher Columbus

"He had a lot to answer for!" proclaimed the Sixth Doctor to Peri in "The Two Doctors" (1985).

John F. Kennedy

Finally, a name-drop from River Song as she claimed in "The Wedding of River Song" (2011) that she used her hallucinogenic lipstick on the president.

Honorable Mention

- Genghis Khan in "Rose" (2005), "The Daemons" (1971), "Marco Polo" (1964), and the 1996 TV Movie
- Hans Christian Andersen in "The Romans" (1965)
- Virginia Woolf in "The Time of Angels" (2010)
- Casanova in "The Vampires of Venice" (2010)

- Michelangelo and Pablo Picasso in "Vincent and the Doctor" (2010)
- Horatio Nelson in "The Sea Devils" (1972)
- Marie Antoinette in "Pyramids of Mars" (1975)
- Florence Nightingale in "The Masque of Mandragora" (1976)
- Galileo in "The Sun Makers" (1977)
- David Lloyd George in "Aliens of London" (2005)

Thank You, Sir, Can I Have a Double?

One of the most-used themes in *Doctor Who* is look-alikes—be it carbon-based similarity or robo-copy. The Time Lord and his companions have had to face versions of themselves and of others many, many times.

"The Day of the Doctor" (2013)

The Zygons created doppelgangers of UNIT staff (including Osgood and Kate Stewart) in order to infiltrate the organization. By extension, this could mean that "The Power of Three" (2012) also featured copies, as it had the suckery aliens.

"The Name of the Doctor" (2013)

A duplicate of Dr. Simeon was recreated by the Great Intelligence.

"Asylum of the Daleks" and "The Snowmen" (2012)

Technically, the Claras in these episodes were doubles of current companion Clara.

"Let's Kill Hitler" and "The Wedding of River Song" (2011)

The Teselecta was used to make mechanical matches of Amy Pond, among others, in the former episode and the Eleventh Doctor in the latter.

"The Rebel Flesh"/"The Almost People" (2011)

Ganger versions of many of the characters were made, including the Doctor and Amy (who, in fact, was a ganger for all the Series 6 episodes leading up to this two-parter).

"The Pandorica Opens"/"The Big Bang" (2010)

Auton Rory!

"Journey's End" (2008)

Two Tenth Doctors! Ten and the Meta-Crisis Doctor, or 10.5 as some call him.

"The Sontaran Stratagem"/"The Poison Sky" (2008)

The spud-like aliens from Sontar created a clone of Martha Jones (along with a few others) in order to infiltrate UNIT. They should get in touch with the Zygons.

"Rise of the Cybermen"/"The Age of Steel" (2006)

In the parallel world, which became known as Pete's World, there were two Mickeys, though one was called "Ricky." You'll find a different Pete and Jackie Tyler there, too.

"Aliens of London"/"World War III" and "Boom Town" (2005)

The Slitheen didn't make doubles, as such, they simply used skin suits and tech to impersonate various members of parliament, the police, and the army.

"Rose" (2005)

Auton Mickey!

Classic *Who* Doppelgangers

- Versions of the **Fifth Doctor** are produced in "The Caves of Androzani" (1984), "Resurrection of the Daleks" (1984), "Arc of Infinity" (1983), and "The King's Demons," (1983) while "Black Orchid" (1982) saw the very likeness of **Nyssa** in Ann Talbot

- The **Fourth Doctor** is reproduced in "Meglos" (1980) and "The Android Invasion" (1975), while "The Androids Of Tara" (1978) featured a **Romana** double and "Terror of the Zygons" (1975) had the **Zygons** up to their facsimile tricks for the first time

- The **Third Doctor's** time in the TARDIS included double trouble in "The Claws of Axos" (1971), "Inferno" (1970), and "Spearhead from Space" (1970)

- The **Second Doctor** came up against himself in "The Enemy of the World" (1967) and a copy of companion **Polly** in "The Faceless Ones" (1967)

- And the **First Doctor** fought against a robot version of his good self in "The Chase" (1965) and a doppelganger in the form of the Abbot in "The Massacre of St Bartholomew's Eve" (1966), while "The Aztecs" (1964) had companion **Barbara** mistaken for the goddess Yetaxa

The Doctor's Fellow Scientists

The Doctor often thinks of himself as a scientist, for whatever reason, and the Gallifreyan seems to attract his fair share of them—both good and bad. So check out some of the more remarkable professors, boffins, geologists, doctors, and weirdos below!

Professor Rachel Jensen

This go-getter helped the Seventh Doctor when two competing Dalek factions were trying to utilize the Hand of Omega in 1963 London, during "Remembrance of the Daleks" (1988). She was instantly taken with the Time Lord's knowledge, trusting him implicitly with his familiarity of their enemy and alien tech. Aided by assistant Allison Williams, the pair were a tad disrespectful of their commanding officer, Group Captain "Chunky" Gilmore, often indulging in impersonations of the man and hi-jinx behind his back. Interestingly, Professor Jensen was familiar with Bernard Quatermass of the British Rocket Group. Her promised memoirs have never appeared...

Todd

Human female Todd met the Fifth Doctor on the luscious jungle world of Deva Loka in the 1982 story "Kinda." The two struck it off immediately as they faced, firstly, the terror of Hindle's deranged "You Can't Mend People" rants and then, secondly, the mystery of the box of Jhana (not to mention the huge, floppy snake, the Mara). Todd's sympathetic side—her almost motherly feelings toward the Kinda—gained the admiration and attention of the Doctor, and it's a great pity she chose not to travel in the TARDIS with her new best buddy (the kids could have done with a mother in there).

Malohkeh

This scaly boffin resided with his fellow Silurians under Cwmtaff in Wales, in the 2010 two-parter "The Hungry Earth"/"Cold Blood." Not as nasty as some of his fellow lizards, Mal (as I'm sure his friends called him) liked to examine, pretty closely and sharply, humans brought down into the Silurian city. He got into the Eleventh Doctor's good books by freeing his subjects and alerting his leader to some even more unpleasant shenanigans by Alaya and Restac. Sadly for old Mal, he was killed by the latter, though he did make an appearance in an alternative time line (caused by River Song and the Doctor's Lake Silencio debacle) when he worked for Emperor Churchill.

Sisters Jatt and Casp

These bad girls were up to no good in the year 5000000023, as the Sisters of Plenitude "looked after" the population of New New Yo.. in "New Earth" (2006). And by "looked after," I mean they conducted agonizing experiments on thousands of humans in a secret intensive "care" department of the New New York Hospital. Both died when the zombie-like collection of almost-walking-dead hospital dwellers were set free. That'll learn 'em!

Winfold Hobbes

At first, Hobbes seemed like the perfect pal for the Tenth Doctor—a jolly, old professor who delighted in travel, with a companion, and who was slightly eccentric, as witnessed in the terrifying "Midnight" (2008). However, this possible BFF turned into the bus mate from hell after the vehicle they were both traveling in, on the planet Midnight, was attacked by a most unusual entity. Hobbes was instrumental in the changing opinion of the passengers that saw them turn against the Time Lord, almost booting him out. The professor's scientific credentials most definitely need another appraisal.

Clifford Jones

Handsome, rugged, handsome, thoughtful, and handsome, Clifford caught the eye of companion Jo Grant in "The Green Death" (1973) when a bunch of giant maggots attracted the concern of the Third Doctor in Wales. His "Nuthutch" lifestyle intrigued Grant and the two

quickly fell for one another (despite his initial rather frosty treatment of her), and married soon after. Clifford's eco-ways stayed with him, and he was last seen in the Ascension Islands, picketing an oil rig. Typical handsome-man behavior.

Ida Scott

The lovely Professor Scott tooled downward with the Tenth Doctor into the heart of Krop Tor, a planetoid orbiting a black hole. A brave soul, Ida confided in the Time Lord as they faced almost certain doom in "The Impossible Planet"/"The Satan Pit" (2006), just moments away from the Beast, chatting about her mother, whom she would never see again. She must have done something right, as the Galifreyan saved her, treating her to some oxygen in the TARDIS.

Dr. Rajesh Singh

Sudoku-loving Rajesh (forgive him, it was the mid-noughties) was a Torchwood employee given the task of looking after what turned out to be a Void ship in the Series 2 finale, "Army of Ghosts"/"Doomsday" (2006). The little guy was fascinated by the object that freaked out most who came into contact with it. Rajesh wasn't fooled by Rose's psychic paper ruse, but he didn't live to gloat about it, becoming the first death at the suckers of the Cult of Skaro after their release from the Void ship.

Dr. Ryder

Ryder was working undercover for Friends of the Ood at Ood Operations under the rather unpleasant Klineman Halpen, who dealt in Ood slavery in "Planet of the Ood" (2008). Unfortunately, Ryder's heroic and well-meaning actions were unrewarded as he found himself thrown into the huge Ood brain. In death, however, his lifelong aim was achieved—the Ood were freed.

Eldrad

Is it a man? Is it a woman? Is it an insane crackpot rock god? All of the above! During "The Hand of Fear" (1976), we discovered Eldrad wasn't well-liked by his/her/its people on Kastria (despite using some deft skills to save and nourish its own planet) and was sent into space in an Obliteration Module, where the people of Kastria assumed some kind of obliteration would take place. But this was not to be, as the Fourth Doctor and Sarah Jane Smith discovered Eldrad's hand, which was conveniently sitting in a quarry (an actual quarry, not some alien wasteland). Having waited thousands of years to come back to life, Eldrad displayed all kinds of crazy scientist behavior and tried to hijack the local Nunton Experimental Complex nuclear reactor. Thankfully for the UK, the Time Lord managed to get Eldrad back to Kastria, where his scarf sent the rock-being into oblivion.

The Who's Who of the Daleks

Surprisingly, the Daleks are a bountiful bunch. They're not only robots and automatons, but also sentient creatures with more to say than just "Exterminate!" And their species has spawned a number of interesting characters. Here are some of the more interesting Daleks roaming the universe(s).

The Cult of Skaro

What a rum bunch these guys were—Daleks with names! Jast and Thay were pretty dull, but their buddy turned enemy, Dalek Sec, the black one, proved to be of slightly more interest. He just wanted to be human. Well, not really, but in "Daleks in Manhattan" (2007), he took the evolution of his species a bit too far. His chums weren't too impressed and put an end to it. Most fascinating, though, is Caan, who survived their exploits in "Doomsday" (2006) and "Evolution of the Daleks" (2007) with an Emergency Temporal Shift. He became somewhat unhinged, though, after it was revealed he flew into the heart of the Time War and started to make all sorts of crazy predictions. Caan's partnership with Davros in "The Stolen Earth" and "Journey's End" (2008) should have been the start of a beautiful friendship (or a sitcom, at least). Sadly, neither survived the wrath of the Meta-Crisis Doctor. Or did they…?

Ironsides

Every home needs a Dalek that offers a cup of tea. These polite pepperpots popped up in 2010's "Victory of the Daleks," providing Winston Churchill and his gang with some much needed refreshment. Sadly, they had an ulterior motive and were soon usurped by…

New Dalek Paradigm

Rainbow-colored Daleks! Or, as they are sometimes known, Fatleks. Or Teletubby Daleks. Or Power Ranger Daleks. Ok, let's move on…

The Metaltron

This little guy was an emotional fella. The brilliant 2005 episode "Dalek" showed a softer side to Skaro's finest, displaying pain, mercy, and even love. Chained up and tortured, he took quite a shine to the Ninth Doctor's companion, Rose Tyler (and her helping hand), before going on a murderous rampage. Bless.

Prime Minister of the Daleks

Much like David Cameron, the current UK Prime Minister, the Dalek PM had a dastardly plan that resulted in some good people being surrounded by a lot of bad, bad types. "Asylum of the Daleks" (2012) saw the Parliament of the Daleks send the Eleventh Doctor, Amy, and Rory down to the titular asylum where they came face to face with some of Skaro's less than pleasant denizens. Ultimately, like most politicians, the PM's plan failed and he proved to be quite the letdown.

Oswin Oswald

A shock to everyone who saw "Asylum of the Daleks" (2012) was the fact that Jenna Coleman made an appearance as Oswin Oswald (when we weren't expecting her until Christmas!). More shocking, however, was when the soufflé-loving future companion turned out to be a Dalek! Still, she made up for it in the end, saving the Doctor and wiping his history from the collective Dalek memory.

Rusty

Or the "Good Dalek." Or the one with morals, according to the Twelfth Doctor in "Into the Dalek" (2014). Capaldi's incarnation met this enigmatic fellow on board the *Aristotle*, a rebel ship fighting the salacious Skarosians. First he was good, and then he was bad. Then he was good again! Rusty, named after former show runner Russell T. Davies (who donated one of his very own Daleks for use in 2012's "Asylum of the Daleks"), realized the Doctor was a good Dalek.

Special Weapons Dalek

This guy doesn't mess around—he doesn't like to chat, he likes to explode (other things, and sometimes himself). His first appearance in "Remembrance of the Daleks" (1988) cemented his status in fandom, leading to a cameo in "Asylum of the Daleks" (2012).

Stone Dalek

Or "River Song's Scaredy-Cat Dalek" as some of us call him. What was the deal with this guy? In 2010's "The Big Bang," this calcified Skaro relic capitulated faster than a Raston Warrior Robot, jumping in the air when confronted with River Song—even begging for mercy! For shame, Mr. Dalek, for shame!

Stoopid Dalek

Don't know this guy's name—possibly Keith—but the First Doctor story "The Chase" (1965) demonstrated that not all Daleks were as bright as one another. When asked to "compute time lag by Earth scale," one Dalek was reduced to a stuttering wreck, even saying "er," while later on, when asked how long, the idiot fumbled, "Er, er, in Earth time, er, four minutes." That is one stoopid Dalek.

Top 10 Most-Featured Companions

Here it is, a companion face-off. Let's find out which companion was the best. Or longest-staying, at least. We haven't included any flashbacks or anything of that nature—just honest to goodness on-screen time (in hours).

10. Susan

The Doctor's very first companion was also his granddaughter, Susan. During her time in the TARDIS (from 1963's "An Unearthly Child" to 1964's "The Dalek Invasion of Earth"), she clocked in fifty-one episodes (with only two off for holidays during filming of 1964's "The Aztecs"), and then returned for "The Five Doctors" (1983) and made a brief appearance, sort of, in "The Name of the Doctor" (2013). Hours: 22+

■ Rose

Rose Tyler was the first companion of the show's 2005 return. Billie Piper's Rose was a firm fan favorite and took in twenty-seven episodes before she left in "Doomsday" (2006). Tyler would make cameo appearances in 2008's "Partners In Crime," "The Sontaran Stratagem," and "Midnight," as well as 2009–10's "The End of Time," Part 2 (none of which are included in the tally here), and then properly in 2008's "Turn Left," "The Stolen Earth," and "Journey's End," and 2013's "The Day of the Doctor." (Fact fans will also note that she starred in the 2005 Children in Need seven-minute special.) Hours: 24+

8. Amy

Beating her predecessor by approximately twenty minutes, Amelia Pond shared thirty-three episodes with the Eleventh Doctor (though we've not included 2011's "Closing Time" and "The Doctor, the Widow and the Wardrobe" in the tally). The feisty ginger also made some extra appearances on DVDs and online (2012's "Pond Life" and "Space/Time," for example), and then made a brief but emotional final appearance in the Eleventh Doctor's swan song, "The Time of the Doctor" (2013). Hours: 24+

7. Romana

You might think this is a slight cheat, considering two different actresses played the Time Lady, but Romana is still Romana regardless of regeneration. Between Mary Tamm and Lalla Ward, they shared sixty-six episodes with Tom Baker's Fourth Doctor (with the latter returning briefly for 1983's "The Five Doctors").

Hours: 27+

6. Tegan

Janet Fielding, who played the Australian trolly dolly, is one of two companions to feature in four consecutive seasons during their time in the TARDIS (the other one is number two on this list). From "Logopolis" (1981) to "Resurrection of the Daleks" (1984), Tegan graced sixty-five episodes, including the feature-length 20th Anniversary special, "The Five Doctors" (1983), and the two-parter that saw her leave (both being forty-five-minute episodes). Peter Davison's finale, "The Caves of Androzani" (1984), saw a brief return for her in a specially filmed moment (though that's not been included in the tally here). She also wins on actual time in making *Doctor Who*, having spent almost exactly three years on the show.

Hours: 28+

5. K9

Like Romana, you might think this is sneaky, but everyone loves K9! Right? Despite appearing in different versions over the years, they've been collected here as one. But compiling his time in the TARDIS is slightly more difficult than your normal companion. Despite spending eighty-eight episodes with Tom Baker's Fourth Doctor, K9 didn't actually appear in all of them. Sometimes he had "circuitry corrosion" (as in 1977's "Image of the Fendhal," only appearing briefly in the opening and closing installments), and sometimes his voice was on holiday or not hired for the story (1978's "The Ribos Operation"; 1979's "Power of Kroll", "City of Death," and "Destiny of the Daleks"; and 1980's "The Leisure Hive" all affected). So his total reflects these many absences. The tin dog would return for 2006's "School Reunion" and briefly for 2008's "Journey's End" (though that one has not been included in the total). And let's not forget the first Doctor Who spin-off, *K9 and Company*, as well as his numerous appearances in *The Sarah Jane Adventures* and his very own series, *K9*, which began in 2009. Well, we didn't forget those, but we certainly didn't include them.

Hours: 29+

4. Ian and Barbara

It's getting tight near the top. On the surface it would appear that we had a tie for the number three slot with the original teaching duo of Coal Hill School featuring in seventy-seven episodes, but after some investigation, we discovered that William Russell and Jacqueline Hill (First Doctor companions Ian and Barbara) took the odd holiday from the show (1964's "The Reign of Terror" and "The Sensorites," for example), missing out on approximately three episodes, and, thus consigning themselves to fourth place.

Hours: 30+

3. Jo Grant

Also starring in seventy-seven episodes was the Third Doctor's favorite, Jo Grant. No holidays for her, and, like Ian and Barbara, Jo never returned to *Doctor Who* (though she did make an appearance in *The Sarah Jane Adventures* alongside Matt Smith).

Hours: 32+

2. Sarah Jane Smith

If there were a Queen of Doctor Who, Sarah Jane Smith would surely be it. So many episodes and so many returns! During her time with Jon Pertwee and Tom Baker, the wonderful Elisabeth Sladen starred in eighty episodes and would go on to return in "The Five Doctors" (1983), "School Reunion" (2006) and "The Stolen Earth"/"Journey's End" (2008)—with a brief cameo in "The End of Time," Part 2 (2009–10). Of course, and like the aforementioned K9, S.J. got a spin-off all of her own (after also starring in 1981's *K9 and Company*) in *The Sarah Jane Adventures*, which adds over twenty-three extra hours of Bannerman Road's finest.

Hours: 40+

1. Jamie, 49+ Hours

Topping the list with no questions asked (and no matter how many holidays/sick days he took), Fraser Hines is the clear winner. Spending almost as long on the show as his Doctor, Patrick Troughton, the highlander got 113 episodes under his kilt before having his mind wiped in "The War Games" (1969). And like the Second Doctor, Jamie returned for "The Two Doctors" (1985), after making a very brief cameo as an illusion in 1983's "The Five Doctors" (not included in his tally).

Hours: 49+

Honorable Mention

Handles: That Cyberman head and Matt Smith's companion ended up spending three hundred years with the Eleventh Doctor, making him the longest-serving (within the fiction of the show).

Unseen Characters

What's better than a seen character in *Doctor Who*? An unseen character! The Doctor meets many, many people but we don't have time to
see them all, so we just get the odd mention or name-check. And here
are some of the more memorable.

Wilson

The chief electrician of department store Henrick's had the honor of
being one of the first words uttered in the return of *Doctor Who* in
2005's "Rose." Rose was looking for him in the basement to give him
some lottery money, when she came across some Autons. Sadly, she
would later find out that Wilson was dead. Now, what was the deal
with Derek?

Jim the Fish

This unusual dam-building fella was revealed to be a buddy of both the
Eleventh Doctor and River Song in the 2011 episode "The Impossible
Astronaut."

The Corsair

Poor guy/gal. Though we do actually see some of the Corsair (her/his
arm) in "The Doctor's Wife" (another 2011 story), for the most part he/
she is unseen. The Eleventh Doctor tells Amy and Rory that the Corsair
is a Time Lord, "one of the good ones," while cheekily adding, "she was
a bad girl" when female.

The Terrible Zodin

Once described as a "woman of rare guile and devilish cunning,"
Zodin was first mentioned in "The Five Doctors" (1983) by the
Second Doctor to the Brigadier, and then again in "Attack of the
Cybermen" (1985), where we learned the Sixth Doctor mistaken-
ly referred to Peri as Zodin in his post-regenerative haze.

The Child Princess of Patrival Regency Nine

"Smith and Jones" (2007) saw the Judoon track down the Plasmavore
who killed this poor girl boasting "pink cheeks and those blond curls
and that simpering voice." Florence, the Plasmavore in question, was
quite proud of her actions.

Tony Tyler

Instead of calling her son Doctor, as she'd teased, Jackie Tyler named
her son Tony. The momentous occasion between the feisty "blond"

and Pete Tyler came at some point between "Doomsday" (2006) and "Journey's End" (2008).

The Could've Been King

Ooooh, this sounds nasty. While facing off against Rassilon in "The End of Time" (2010), the Tenth Doctor told his BFF, the Master, that the time-lock on the Time War would release all sorts of horrors, including the Could've Been King with his army of Meanwhiles and Never-weres.

Shareen

For someone never seen, Shareen does get a lot of mentions. A chum of Rose, she's referred to in "The End of the World" (2005), where Miss Tyler quoted her; "The Unquiet Dead" (2005), where she tells Gwyneth she would look at boys with Shareen; "Aliens of London" (2005), where Rose claimed she'd stayed the night at Shareen's, only to discover she'd been away for a year; and "School Reunion" (2006), where she tells Sarah Jane Smith that the only time she fell out with Shareen was "over a man." We salute you, Shareen!

I.M. Foreman

Right from the very first episode, Doctor Who has tantalized us with unseen characters. The name I.M. Foreman can be seen emblazoned on the doors of the 76 Totter's Lane junkyard in "An Unearthly Child" (1966), "Attack of the Cybermen" (1985), and the 50th Anniversary special, "The Day of the Doctor" (2013).

10 *Doctor Who* References in *Torchwood*

You might not know this, but Torchwood was first mentioned in the 2005 episode "Bad Wolf" (and numerous times after), and got its own spin-off series starring John Barrowman as the gregarious and omnisexual Captain Jack Harkness. So far, four seasons have aired, each teeming with references to its mother show. Here are ten of the best.

1. *Children of Earth,* "Day One"
Plenty here to choose from in the third season of adventures for Jack and his chums. Look out for name-checks for Colonel Mace (2008's "The Sontaran Stratagem"), companion Martha Jones, and UNIT. Actor Peter Capaldi (currently wowing audiences as the Twelfth Doctor) stars as government pawn Frobisher which was also the name of the Sixth Doctor's shape-shifting penguin companion in the *Doctor Who Magazine* comic strips.

2. *Miracle Day,* "The Blood Line"
The finale for the fourth season, mainly set in North America, included a number of nods, including the Doctor, Silurians, and the Racnoss.

3. "Small Worlds"
This tremendous and haunting first season story had Fifth Doctor fans excited with Captain Jack remembering the Mara, who first appeared in "Kinda" (1982).

4. *Children of Earth,* "Day Three"
Yay! Look out, it's newsreader Trinity Wells! After many appearances in *Doctor Who,* she gets to crossover covering the news as always. (Fact fans will also note the presence of the French newsreader who has popped up in *Who,* too.)

5. "Captain Jack Harkness"
This penultimate season one tale includes Bad Wolf graffiti, a "Vote Saxon" poster, and Jack talking about the events of "The Parting of the Ways" (2005).

6. "Exit Wounds"
Scientist Toshiko Sato reveals that she faced the Slitheen's space pig in "Aliens of London" (2005) instead of Torchwood colleague Owen,

as he was hungover. Also, there's a blink-and-you'll-miss-it glimpse of a Hoix—which first appeared in "Love & Monsters" (2006).

7. *Miracle Day,* **"Immortal Sins"**

Episode seven of the fourth season saw Jack mention the Trickster's Brigade—the nasty gang behind Donna Noble's parallel universe antics in "Turn Left" (2008). The Trickster was a regular enemy in the other spin-off series, *The Sarah Jane Adventures* (where, fact fans will note, the evil entity faced off against the Tenth Doctor).

8. **"Adam"**

Listen carefully for the Void, as featured in "Doomsday" (2006).

9. *Children of Earth,* **"Day Five"**

Gwen Cooper, who appeared in "The Stolen Earth"/"Journey's End" (2008), laments the absence of the Doctor as the world comes to an end.

10. **"End of Days"**

Excitingly, the finale for the first season ends with the sound of the TARDIS filling the Torchwood Hub in Cardiff. The events of "Utopia" (2007) would follow on directly from this story. Also of note is a reference to Abaddon, son of the Beast (2006's "The Impossible Planet"/"The Satan Pit"),

Honorable Mention

- Captain Jack's Vortex Manipulator

- The Tenth Doctor's hand in a jar (which would return to *Doctor Who* in the Series 3 episode "Utopia")

- Numerous references to the Battle of Canary Wharf, Cybermen, and the Rift

- Companion Martha Jones shows up for some fun with the Cardiff-based gang

50 Things to Note When Rewatching "The Day of the Doctor"

The record-breaking 50th Anniversary special had a lot of things to look out for, referencing so many eras and moments from the Doctor's past (and even his future!). Here are just fifty of them (there are many, many more in the episode itself).

1. The opening titles are just like they were in the sixties!

2. Menacing policeman: a neat nod to the first episode, "An Unearthly Child" (1963).

3. I.M. Foreman: a return to Totter's Lane where the show first began.

4. Coal Hill School: again, used in the very first story.

5. Chesterton and Coburn are names on the school sign: the former being Ian's surname and the latter the surname of the first episode's writer.

6. Clara leaves school at 17:16, the time when "An Unearthly Child" (1963) was broadcast.

7. Clara snaps the TARDIS doors shut. The Tenth Doctor first did this in "Forest of the Dead" (2008).

8. Kate Stewart's phone makes the TARDIS dematerialization noise.

9. A couple of references to Malcolm, the UNIT scientist from "Planet of the Dead" (2009).

10. Osgood's scarf: a reference to Tom Baker ("Nice scarf," says the Doctor).

11. Osgood: possibly related to UNIT technician Osgood from "The Daemons" (1971).

12. Elizabeth I helps out in the adventure, and she marries the Tenth Doctor, too. "I will be right back," he coos, but won't see her again for many years in her time line in "The Shakespeare Code" (2007); hence why she wasn't too pleased.

13. The Doctor mentions working for UNIT, which he did when he was the Third Doctor (Jon Pertwee).

I.M.FOREMAN

BAD
WOLF

Geronimo!

1716231163

timey-wimey

14. The Fall of Arcadia: first mentioned by the Tenth Doctor in "Doomsday" (2006).

15. The High Council is holding an emergency session: we see this in "The End of Time" (2009–10).

16. The Omega Arsenal: Omega was a Time Lord first encountered in "The Three Doctors" (1972–73).

17. The Moment: first mentioned in "The End of Time" (2009–10).

18. When the War Doctor approaches the Space Barn, his surroundings are very similar to the "alien sand and hear the cries of strange birds" mentioned by the First Doctor in "An Unearthly Child" (1963).

19. The War Doctor laments the lack of a big red button on the Moment. The Doctor can't resist a "great big threatening button," as revealed in "The Christmas Invasion" (2005).

20. The Moment says "Bad Wolf" —the Ninth Doctor season arc.

21. Fez: the Eleventh's favorite headgear of choice making its last appearance in *Doctor Who*.

22. It's a Zygon! First seen in "Terror of the Zygons" (1975), this appearance is their first proper on-screen return to *Doctor Who*.

23. "Geronimo!": the Eleventh Doctor's catchphrase.

24. The Doctors calling each other derogatory names: a tradition that began in "The Three Doctors" (1972–73) and carried on in every multi-Doctor story since.

25. Kate asks Malcolm for a file code-named Cromer. Cromer is where The Brigadier, her father, thought they had been transported to in "The Three Doctors" (1972–73).

26. According to Kate, the Cromer file will be found either in the seventies or eighties, "depending on the dating protocol"—a reference to "UNIT dating," a problem occurred when trying to accurately pin down when UNIT stories took place. All due to the dating of "Mawdryn Undead" (1983).

27. The expression "reverse the polarity" gets another outing: first used in "The Sea Devils" (1972).

28. On discovering there are three Doctors, Kate says, "There's a precedent for that," referencing her father's outings in the multi-Doctor

stories, "The Three Doctors" (1972–73) and "The Five Doctors" (1983).

29. Much to John Hurt's disgust, the phrase "timey-wimey" also gets another outing. First used in "Blink" (2007).

30. The Black Archive contains photographs of the Doctor's known associates and companions. And even Kamelion. Interestingly, there are a lot of BBC promotional publicity pics in there. UNIT must have connections.

31. Captain Jack's vortex manipulator makes a return. Its activation code is 1716231163; the first episode, "An Unearthly Child," aired at 17:16 on 23.11.63.

32. Captain Grumpy asks, "Is there a lot of this in the future?" in reference to kissing. "It does start to happen," comes the reply from Eleven. This is a knowing nod to the fact that some fans of the classic series aren't too keen on PDA.

33. The Doctors note the "round things" in the TARDIS, often known as "roundels." Whatever you call them, they don't seem to have much use.

34. The TARDIS console's friction contrafibulator makes an appearance, first seen in "Vincent and the Doctor" (2010).

35. The Tenth Doctor sighs, "Oh, you've redecorated. I don't like it," on seeing the new TARDIS interior. The Second Doctor didn't like the new TARDIS in "The Three Doctors" (1972–73) or the Brigadier's new office in "The Five Doctors" (1983), just as the Eleventh Doctor didn't like Craig Owen's new place in "Closing Time" (2011).

36. The Black Archive contains River Song's red shoes, as seen in "The Time of Angels" (2010).

37. The Black Archive contains Magna Clamps, as used in "Army of Ghosts"/"Doomsday" (2006).

38. The Black Archive contains Amelia Pond's red pinwheel, as seen in "The Eleventh Hour" (2010).

39. The space-time telegraph is seen: the Brigadier used it to contact the Fourth Doctor in "Terror of the Zygons."

40. The Black Archive contains a Clockwork Droid facemask, first seen in "The Girl in the Fireplace" (2006).

41. The Black Archive contains a Dalek tommy gun, as used in "Evolution of the Daleks" (2007).

42. The Black Archive contains the heads of Supreme Dalek (as seen in 2008's "The Stolen Earth"/"Journey's End") and a Cyberman. (There's also a lot more to see in the Black Archive!)

43. The Moment describes the sound of the TARDIS as "wheezing, groaning," two words regularly used by Terrance Dicks in the *Doctor Who* Target novelizations.

44. *All* of the Doctors! Even a future one (Peter Capaldi).

45. John Hurt's War Doctor says, "Wearing a bit thin," with regards to his oncoming regeneration, just as the First Doctor did in "The Tenth Planet" (1966).

46. The War Doctor also says, "I hope the ears are a bit less conspicuous this time": a cheeky nod to the fact his successor, the Ninth Doctor, as played by Christopher Eccleston, would have noticeable ears.

47. Ten says to Eleven, "Good to know my future is in safe hands." The First Doctor says the same to the Fifth Doctor in "The Five Doctors" (1983).

48. Sticking with the Tenth Doctor just as he leaves his new BFF, he says, "I don't want to go." These were his last words in "The End of Time" (2009–10).

49. The Curator. The Tom Baker.

50. The Doctor's faces in the end titles. A first for the show as we're normally treated to just one in the opening (depending on year).

7 Classic Series In-Jokes

Doctor Who has been full of lovely self-references and in-jokes over the years—some obvious, some not so obvious (and some probably the result of a bored mind). Collected here are some personal favorites from the classic era.

"The Robots of Death" (1977)

Poul, that *poor* bastard. Thankfully, in the 2010s, nobody suffers from "robophobia," though I think the Church of England may have something to say about it (and robosexuals). But back in the 1970s, it went under the name "Grimwade's Syndrome." Which sounds pretty nasty, to be honest.

Of course, some of you may know that the use of "Grimwade" was actually a reference to then-production assistant (and future director of stories such as "Kinda" and "Earthshock," and writer of "Mawdryn Undead," among others) Peter Grimwade. Apparently, his first wife was, wait for it, a robot.

"The Greatest Show in the Galaxy" (1988)

"I've got all sorts of souvenirs. All the posters. I had a long correspondence with one of the founder members too, soon after it started. Although I never got to see the early days, I know it's not as good as it used to be but I'm still terribly interested."

Sound familiar? Yup, Whizz Kid was the archetypal *Doctor Who* fan (just check out that bow tie for timey-wimey, wibbly-wobbly-ness) with his "it's not as good as it used to be" mantra and collect-everything-he-can mentality. In 1988, it was quite timely, as fandom hadn't been so fannish for that long. Spot on from the production team. Some years later, "The God Complex" (2011) would imitate this character, somewhat less successfully due to the fact that *Who* fans seemed to have moved on (though I'm sure some do still exist in that fashion). Also worth pointing out is that Ace tries on Tom Baker's scarf and one of Mel's costumes for more in-gaggery from "The Greatest Show in the Galaxy" (1988–89).

"The Ribos Operation" (1978)

Back in the seventies, Tom Baker liked the odd drink. During one of his sojourns, he managed to find his lip on the receiving end of a dog bite the night before filming on the first part of The Key to Time season was to take place. Action had to be taken to explain his disfigurement.

And this is why we see the Fourth Doctor bang his mouth on the TARDIS console at the beginning of this story!

"Destiny of the Daleks" (1979)

There's a neat *Hitchhikers' Guide to the Galaxy* gag in here (author Douglas Adams was *Doctor Who*'s script editor at the time), but you can find out more about that in the TV Shows That *Doctor Who* References list (see page 126). What is worth noting is Romana's *Pretty Woman*–esque regeneration fashion show at the start, in which she tried out some new bodies, only to land on Princess Astra, last seen in the previous story, "The Armageddon Factor"—mainly down to the fact that they were played by the same actress, Lalla Ward. Also, Romana's costume is a female version of the Fourth Doctor's, complete with scarf.

"The Trial of a Time Lord" (1986)

Not so much an in-joke as a comment on the state of the show at that time. Michael Grade, who was in charge of the BBC, wanted to get rid of *Doctor Who*. After an eighteen-month hiatus, the show returned in an effort to prove itself, and so the good Doctor was on trial in and outside of the show.

"The Hand of Fear" (1976)

Throughout the years, *Doctor Who* production has often utilized the odd quarry as an alien landscape. But here, it's an actual quarry. Instead of finding themselves in South Croydon (which sounds slightly worse), the Doctor says, somewhat knowingly, "We're in a quarry." How meta!

"Remembrance of the Daleks" (1988)

"This is BBC television, the time is quarter past five, and Saturday viewing continues with an adventure in the new science fiction series *Do…*"

Dot to Dot? Dorothy in Space? Just what was the name of that show the announcer was about to blurt out as the Seventh Doctor companion, Ace, was leaving the house? Given that the story is set in 1963, we can guess. (Yet, pedants note: it's quite bright outside for November at teatime, yes?) It's certainly the most brazen and obvious of the in-jokes here, though many are critical of its placement within the story. But given that it was broadcast in an anniversary year (the 25th), we can forgive them such a shoehorned clanger.

7 New Series In-Jokes

Earlier on we looked at in-jokes in the world of classic *Doctor Who*; now it's the turn of the new series. (Just to add, "The Day of the Doctor" gets its own special section on page xx).

"The Poison Sky" (2008)

A nice, quick, and obvious one to kick off with. "The Poison Sky" very specifically referenced 2005's "The Empty Child" with David Tennant's Doctor asking a bemused Colonel Mace, "Are you my mummy?" Oddly, he doesn't reply or ask, "What you talkin' about, Willis?" Mind you, we wouldn't have heard him if he had, due to our collective guffaws.

"The Bells of Saint John" (2013)

If you've visited London, England, you may have taken a trip to Earls Court and noticed a very familiar blue police box outside. Sadly, it's not a real TARDIS (apparently), and as we see in this episode, others thought it was real, too. "Earls Court was an embarrassment," moans one baddie in search for the Doctor. Fact fans will note that Google Street View has a treat in store for you if you check the police box out there.

"The Stolen Earth" (2008)

This joke wouldn't really have worked with Peter Davison at the helm: "Saturday! Good! Good. I like Saturdays!" proclaims the Tenth Doctor (despite it being the end of the universe—apparently). Can't imagine The Fifth Doctor saying, "I like Mondays!" Anyway, it's a knowing nod to the very day that *Doctor Who* is synonymous with—for many of us, the show is the very essence of Saturday—and a great way to kick off a finale.

Also, fans of "spatial genetic multiplicity" had a chortle when the Gwen Cooper/Gwyneth conundrum was finally answered.

"The End of Time" Part Two (2010)

Now, there are a lot of references to the past here, but the one that really counts is David Tennant's almost final words to the *lurve* of his life, Billie Piper. Staggering against a wall like a *Who* fan meeting John Barrowman at a convention, the Doctor tells her, "I bet you're gonna have a really great year," after she says it's 2005. Of course, we all had a really great year that year. *sniff* #memories

"Blink" (2007)

In a world where pop culture T-shirts are made instantly and without a second's thought (or imagination), along comes Steven Moffat to show off his street smartz. As soon as his 2005 episode "The Empty Child" aired, a tee was made (by a fan) with "Are You My Mummy?" emblazoned on it—and look what he did in "Blink." As soon as we hear the Doctor say, "The angels have the phone box," Larry Nightingale purrs, "I've got that on a T-shirt." It's a funny line in its own right, but there's added giggles for those in the know.

"Blink" also gets extra in-gag points for the almost hilarious "wrong size windows on the TARDIS" one-liner. "Fans" had debated on an Internet forum (don't go there, kids, only bad things happen there) that the new TARDIS windows were of incorrect dimensions (as I say, don't go there unless window-measuring is something you're particularly keen on). Moffat, ever the wag (and one-time forum dweller), picked up on this and prepped his acerbic penmanship to eviscerate these "humans."

"The Snowmen" (2010)

There are a few knowing gags going on here, possibly. We'll get the casting of two-time Doctor Who, though never actually a "proper" one, Richard E. Grant (2003's *Scream of the Shalka*, 1999's "The Curse of Fatal Death") out of the way, as it's tenuous at best.

But let's take a look at Clara's entrance into the TARDIS and the Doctor's expectant, almost smug, face waiting to hear that line for the first time again. It's like he's us! But good old Clara is too smart for that (or maybe Steven Moffat is) and beams that the Time Lord's ship is "smaller on the outside!" Not only a fabulous tip to forty-nine years and a bit of "*Who*story," but an amazing joke from Moffat.

And then there's her gravestone. We're assuming you all freeze-framed it like we did and studied the date? Well, in case you're not like us, she was born on November 23. Blimey. That's a coincidence! #smirk

"Human Nature" (2007)

And here's my personal favourite, and perhaps the most touching of them all. More of a tribute than an in-joke, two of the creators of *Doctor Who*, Verity Lambert and Sydney Newman, are honoured. While in human form, the Tenth Doctor tells his latest squeeze, Joan Redfern, about his parents: "Sidney was a watchmaker from Nottingham, and my mother Verity was, er. Well, she was a nurse, actually." Later, in "The End of Time" Part Two (2010), we would see that Joan's great-granddaughter was called Verity Newman. Beautiful.

Actors Who Appear in Classic and New *Who*

Though seemingly worlds apart at times, the classic run (1963–1989) does share a number of actors and actresses with the new series (2005 onward). Below you'll find all those who've made this illustrious list.

Tom Baker
The Fourth Doctor and the Curator in "The Day of the Doctor" (2013).

Peter Davison
The Fifth Doctor and back for "Time Crash" (2007).

Elisabeth Sladen
Sarah Jane Smith in the Tom Baker era (and in 1983's "The Five Doctors") and back again for "School Reunion" (2006), "The Stolen Earth"/"Journey's End" (2008), and "The End of Time" Part Two (2010).

Brian Miller
Elisabeth's husband, Brian, made a memorable debut in "Snakedance" (1983) while also providing Dalek voices in "Resurrection of the Daleks" (1984) and "Remembrance of the Daleks" (1988). Miller starred as Barney in "Deep Breath" (2014) and also made an appearance in *The Sarah Jane Adventures*' story "The Mad Woman in the Attic" (2009).

John Leeson
K9 in the Tom Baker era and back for "School Reunion" (2006) and "The Stolen Earth"/"Journey's End" (2008).

Trevor Laird
Frax in episodes 5–8 of "The Trial of a Time Lord" (1986) and Clive Jones in "Smith and Jones" and "The Sound of Drums"/"The Last of the Time Lords" (all 2007).

David Troughton
Patrick's son was a guard in "The Enemy of the World" (1967–68), Private Moor in "The War Games" (1966), King Peladon in "The Curse of Peladon" (1972), and Professor Hobbes in "Midnight" (2008).

Lynda Baron
Captain Wrack in "Enlightenment" (1983) and Val in "Closing Time" (2011). Fact fans will note that she was the voice behind "The Ballad of the Last Chance Saloon" in "The Gunfighters" (1966).

Christopher Benjamin

Sir Keith Gold in "Inferno" (1970), Jago in "The Talons of Weng-Chiang" (1977), and Colonel Hugh in "The Unicorn and the Wasp" (2008).

Christopher Ryan

Kiv in episodes 5–8 of "The Trial of a Time Lord" (1986), General Staal in "The Sontaran Stratagem"/"The Poison Sky" (2008), and Commander Stark in "The Pandorica Opens" (2010).

Trevor Cooper

Takis in "Revelation of the Daleks" (1985) and back for some Merry Men fun in "Robot of Sherwood" (2014).

Pauline Collins

Samantha Briggs in "The Faceless Ones" (1967) and Queen Victoria in "Tooth and Claw" (2006).

Colin Spaul

Lilt in "Revelation of the Daleks" (1985) and Mr. Crane in "Rise of the Cybermen"/"The Age of Steel" (2006).

Clive Swift

Jobel in "Revelation of the Daleks" (1985) and Mr. Copper in "Voyage of the Damned" (2007).

Annie Reid

Nurse Crane in "The Curse of Fenric" (1989) and Florence Finnegan in "Smith and Jones" (2007).

Geoffrey Palmer

Masters in "Doctor Who and the Silurians" (1970), Administrator in "The Mutants" (1972), and Hardaker in "Voyage of the Damned" (2007).

Marc Warren

Uncredited extra in "Battlefield" (1989) and Elton in "Love & Monsters" (2006).

David Warwick

Kimus in "The Pirate Planet" and Police Commissioner in "Army of Ghosts"/"Doomsday" (2006). Fact fans will note that he is also Louise Jameson's husband.

Gabriel Woolf

Sutekh in "Pyramids of Mars" (1975) and the voice of The Beast in "The Impossible Planet"/"The Satan Pit" (2006).

William Thomas

Martin in "Remembrance of the Daleks" (1988) and Cleaver in "Boom Town" (2005). Fact fans will also note that he plays Gwen Cooper's dad, Geraint, in the spin-off series *Torchwood*.

Arthur Cox

Cully in "The Dominators" (1968) and Mr. Henderson in "The Eleventh Hour" (2010).

Garrick Hagon

Ky in "The Mutants" (1972) and Abraham in "A Town Called Mercy" (2012).

Margaret John

Megan Jones in "Fury from the Deep" (1968) and Grandma Connolly in "The Idiot's Lantern" (2006).

Nick Hobbs

Various credited and uncredited roles in the early seventies and Mr. Nainby in "Amy's Choice" (2010).

Louis Mahoney

Newscaster in "Frontier in Space" (1973), Ponti in "Planet of Evil" (1975), and Billy Shipton (older version) in "Blink" (2007).

Jessica Martin

Mags in "The Greatest Show in the Galaxy" (1988–89) and the voice of Queen Elizabeth II in "Voyage of the Damned" (2007).

Nisha Nayar

Red Kang in "Paradise Towers" (1987) and Female Programmer in "Bad Wolf"/"The Parting of the Ways" (2005).

Sheila Reid

Etta in "Vengeance on Varos" (1985) and Clara's grandmother in "The Time of the Doctor" (2013).

Daphne Oxenford

Archivist in "Dragonfire" (1987) and Agatha Christie (older version) in "The Unicorn and the Wasp" (2008). Fact fans will note that this scene was cut from the broadcast episode.

Honorable Mention

- *Doctor Who* Series 8 saw old-timers **Trevor Cooper** (1985's "Revelation of the Daleks") and **Tony Osoba** (1979's "Destiny of the Daleks" and 1987's "Dragonfire") return to the show.

- **Katy Manning**, who played Jo Grant in the Jon Pertwee era, returned in *The Sarah Jane Adventures* story "Death of the Doctor" (2010).

10 World Landmarks Featured in *Doctor Who*

We all know that the Doctor likes the odd visit to Earth now and again, and occasionally there'll be a very familiar building or monument featured in Doctor Who. Here you'll find ten of the best from the Time Lord's travels on our planet (London gets its own special entry on page 57).

The White House
Washington, D.C.'s seat of power has cropped up a number of times in recent years. We caught a fleeting glimpse of it from outside shortly before President Obama got his face changed into that of John Simm in "The End of Time" (2009–10) and a another snatch in "The Power of Three" (2012). But it was in the Series 6 opener, "The Impossible Astronaut"/"Day of the Moon" (2011) where we got the best look inside the president's home.

Eiffel Tower
Unsurprisingly, the beautiful tower featured large in Doctor Who's first filming outside of the UK. In "City of Death" (1979), the Fourth Doctor and Romana took in the view and got all ostentatious, and then flew back down. The Eiffel Tower could also be briefly spotted in the 1996 TV Movie, "Army of Ghosts"/"Doomsday" (2006), and "The Power of Three" (2012).

Millennium Centre
Definitely one of the buildings in the UK everyone should visit. And not just because *Doctor Who* actually filmed in there (in 2006's "New Earth" and 2011's "The Girl Who Waited," for example). On his visits to the Welsh city of Cardiff, you'll find the impressive building in the background of episodes such as "Boom Town" (2005) and "The Last of the Time Lords" (2007).

Empire State Building
This is one of the first landmarks outside of the UK to make an appearance in *Doctor Who*. Back in 1965, the New York building appeared in the First Doctor six-parter "The Chase," while it would reappear again in 2007's "Daleks in Manhattan"/"Evolution of the Daleks" (where Skaro's finest used it in their evil plot), "The Stolen Earth" (2008), and "The Angels Take Manhattan" (2012).

Sydney Opera House

A blink-and-you'll-miss-it appearance from the Australian building, but look closely and you'll see the Eleventh Doctor there with Kazran Sardick and Abigail Pettigrew in "A Christmas Carol" (2010).

Stonehenge

The stone circle received a mention by the Monk in "The Time Meddler" (1965) and briefly appeared in the 1996 TV Movie with the Eighth Doctor, but it wasn't until the Eleventh Doctor's showdown with the Alliance (that ended with him in the Pandorica and rebooting the universe) in "The Pandorica Opens"/"The Big Bang" (2010) that we got a good old look at Stonehenge.

Statue of Liberty

Back to New York again and Lady Liberty made a quick appearance in 1965's "The Chase" (albeit on a monitor) and also in the 1996 TV Movie before making a proper appearance in "Daleks in Manhattan"/"Evolution of the Daleks" (2007) and then more sinisterly in the Ponds' farewell, "The Angels Take Manhattan" (2012)—where she clomped over New York City.

Taj Mahal

In "Army of Ghosts"/"Doomsday" (2006), the Cybermen could be seen appearing beside the marvelous mausoleum in India. Fact fans will note that the very same footage was used again a few years later in "The Power of Three" (2012).

Extra! Extra!

 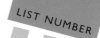

There are scores of *Doctor Who* DVDs and Blu-rays out there and each come packed with amazing special features, such as TV show appearances, commentaries, and isolated music scores. Here are some of the very finest extras you can find in the world of *Who* DVDs. (Note that some of these extras aren't necessarily available in all regions or editions, so check your versions carefully!)

"Night and the Doctor" (2011)

These five fun scenes see great interaction between Matt Smith, Alex Kingston, Karen Gillan, and Arthur Darvill as the Eleventh Doctor, River Song, Amy, and Rory ask interesting questions of the Time Lord in the TARDIS. It also features a goldfish. Available on *The Complete Sixth Series*.

William Hartnell Interview

Hartnell, who played the First Doctor, has somewhat of a reputation for being slightly grumpy. And this recently discovered interview from 1967, just a year after he left *Doctor Who*, does nothing to contradict this fact, with the actor in rather tetchy form. Available on *The Tenth Planet*.

Invisible TARDIS Deleted Scene

"Terror of the Zygons" (1975) didn't need much selling to fans, being an absolute classic story, but the inclusion of a never-before-seen deleted scene sweetened the deal. Featuring Tom Baker, Elisabeth Sladen, and Ian Marter (as the Fourth Doctor, Sarah Jane, and Harry Sullivan, respectively), this amazing moment from the past also includes an invisible TARDIS materialization! Available on *Terror of the Zygons*.

David Tennant's Video Diaries

David Tennant's time as the Tenth Doctor is well documented, but never in so personal and fun way as his own video diaries. His first two series are covered extensively, but it's his very final moments, just before he films his final scenes as the Time Lord, that strike such a potent chord. Barely able to hold back the tears, Tennant makes his way to set to do what he does best. Definitely get tissues before watching. Available on *The Complete Second Series*, *The Complete Third Series*, *The Complete Fourth Series*, and *The Complete Specials*.

TARDIS Coral Deleted Scene

The beach scene near the end of "Journey's End" (2008) originally saw the Tenth Doctor also give Rose a piece of TARDIS coral so that she and her new BF (the Meta-Crisis Doctor) could live happily ever after. Sadly, this was cut out of the broadcast version but is included here in all its epic glory. Available on *The Complete Fourth Series* [CE: Cam needs to add text here in next round]

Mara CGI

Brilliant Fifth Doctor tale "Kinda" (1982) only suffered in one department: a risible rubber, not to mention giant, snake. Thanks to magic and wizardry (i.e., computers), the abomination has been replaced with a stunning bit of CG work, rendering the story utterly perfect. Available on *Mara Tales*.

"The Five Doctors" Commentary

A bit cheeky including this, as it was actually an Easter egg, but this is one extra everyone has to listen to. This audio commentary features David Tennant (who was still playing the Tenth Doctor at the time) and Phil Collinson (likewise, still working on the show) and a more hilarious ninety minutes you are unlikely to find. Seek it out! Available on *The Five Doctors: Special Edition*.

Mark Gatiss Video Diary

While his story "The Unquiet Dead" (2005) made it from script to screen, the lovely Mark Gatiss documented the journey. Like fellow fan Tennant, his love and enthusiasm is palpable. Available on *The Complete First Series*.

Paul McGann Audition

What can one say? An audition, with Paul McGann! Not only that, the script he reads from includes mentions of his "father," Ulysses; his "brother," the Master; and the Scrolls of Rassilon. Mind-blowing! Available on *Revisitations 1*.

Doctor Who's International Filming Locations

Out of the eight hundred or so episodes filmed, only a handful feature scenes that were filmed outside of the UK. Included here are those episodes—some of which were filmed extensively away from *Doctor Who's* home, as it were, and others featuring very brief moments filmed outside the UK.

Paris, France
"City of Death" (1979)
Amsterdam, Netherlands
"Arc of Infinity" (1983)
Lanzarote, Canary Islands
"Planet of Fire" (1984)
Seville, Spain
"The Two Doctors" (1985)
Vancouver, Canada
The Paul McGann TV Movie (1996)
New York, United States
"Daleks in Manhattan"/"Evolution of the Daleks" (2007)
Cinecittà Studios, Rome, Italy
"The Fires of Pompeii" (2008)
Dubai, United Arab Emirates
"Planet of the Dead" (2009)
Trogir, Croatia; Venice, Italy
"The Vampires of Venice" (2010)
Trogir, Croatia
"Vincent and the Doctor" (2010)
Utah and Arizona, United States
"The Impossible Astronaut"/"Day of the Moon" (2011)
Sierra Nevada Mountains, Spain
"Asylum of the Daleks" (2012)
Almería, Spain
"A Town Called Mercy" (2012)
New York, United States
The Angels Take Manhattan" (2012)
New York, United States; Japan
"The Bells of Saint John" (2013)
Lanzarote, Canary Islands
Kill the Moon (2014)

London Landmarks

The Doctor does like Earth but, in particular, he hearts London the mostest. From the very first episode in 1963, set in the East End, to the latest series, the Time Lord is always stopping off there. Find below London's most famous and notable buildings and sights featured in *Doctor Who* over the years.

Big Ben and the Houses of Parliament

The classic series wasn't too keen on being flashy and showing well-known landmarks, but these iconic London landmarks have been featured very heavily since the show's 2005 return. Big Ben was a prominent moment of the new series with that classic Space Pig crash in 2005's "Aliens of London" (and the subsequent rebuilding of it in "The Christmas Invasion"). BB would also be most noticeable in "The Empty Child" later that same year, as Rose and Captain Jack Harkness got all dancey in front of it, and as the newly regenerated Matt Smith almost hurt himself on it while flying past, clinging to the TARDIS in "The Eleventh Hour" (2010). Recently, Big Ben had a Tyrannosaurus rex walk past, and the Half Face Man landed on its spire in "Deep Breath" (2014).

You can see these landmarks in many other modern London stories, but you can also find them in older adventures, such as "The Dalek Invasion of Earth" (1964) and the Paul McGann TV Movie (1996). Fact fans will note that in "The Snowmen" (2012), Clara claimed she was born behind Big Ben's clock face.

London Eye

"Round and massive, slap bang in the middle of London. A huge circular metal structure like a dish, like a wheel. Radial. Close to where we're standing. Must be completely invisible," said the Ninth Doctor in "Rose" (2005). (Look closely and you'll also see the TARDIS fly over it in 2010's "The Eleventh Hour.")

St. Paul's Cathedral

The iconic image of the Cybermen marching in front of the historically fascinating domed building in "The Invasion" (1968) is hard to beat. A testament to one of *Doctor Who*'s finest directors, Douglas Camfield. St. Paul's also made an appearance in both the opening episode and finale of Series 8.

The Shard

Though it first appeared in an alternate time line in "The Wedding of River Song" (2011), this latest addition to the London skyline features heavily in 2013's "The Bells of Saint John." Hilariously, the Eleventh Doctor rode an anti-gravity bike up the side of the building in order to defeat Miss Kizlet and her Spoonheads.

Post Office Tower

In the very same year it officially opened, *Doctor Who* honored London's tallest construction (at the time) by placing nasty computer WOTAN in there in "The War Machines" (1966). This Grade II listed building is now called the BT Tower.

Tower of London

The 50th Anniversary special, "The Day of the Doctor," highlighted the landmark beautifully with UNIT and the Black Archive being situated there, though the Tower of London was first seen in 2005's "The Christmas Invasion." Fact fans will note that the Doctor had previously been in the Tower, as mentioned in "The Sensorites" (1964), "The Mind of Evil" (1971), "The Impossible Astronaut" (2011), and, indeed, in the aforementioned "The Day of the Doctor" (three different incarnations!).

Battersea Power Station

Currently undergoing a refurb, this familiar building was first seen in "The Dalek Invasion of Earth" (1964) with half of its famous chimney damaged, and then many years later in an adventure with the Doctor's other foes, the Cybermen. "Rise of the Cybermen"/"Age of Steel" (2006) saw the station used as a Cyber-conversion base.

Stories with "Doctor" in the Title

A nice and simple list here: Doctor Who adventures with Doctor in the title. The first couple listed here are episode titles from multi-part adventures, with the story title given in brackets. It's interesting to note that more than half of these stories are from the 2005 relaunch.

"Death of Doctor Who" ("The Chase," episode 5, 1965)

"A Holiday for the Doctor" ("The Gunfighters," episode 1, 1966)

"The Three Doctors" (1973)

"The Five Doctors" (1983)

"The Two Doctors" (1985)

"Doctor Who" (1996)

"The Doctor Dances" (2005)

"The Doctor's Daughter" (2008)

"The Next Doctor" (2008)

"Vincent and the Doctor" (2010)

"The Doctor's Wife" (2011)

"The Doctor, the Widow and the Wardrobe" (2011)

"The Name of the Doctor" (2013)

"The Day of the Doctor" (2013)

"The Time of the Doctor" (2013)

Honorable Mention

"Death of the Doctor" (2010): the wonderful two-parter from *The Sarah Jane Adventures* featuring Matt Smith.

"Time" in a Title

Among fans, there's often the agreement that any *Who* episode with "Time" in its title is a bit of a stinker. While this sentiment is not true of all of them, some episodes do have a reputation for being, how should we say, less than good. Anyway, judge for yourself. It's interesting that in recent years, both Russell T. Davies and Steven Moffat have veered away from much usage of the word.

"The Dimensions of Time" ("The Space Museum," episode 2, 1965)

"The Death of Time" ("The Chase," episode 2, 1965)

"Destruction of Time" ("The Daleks' Master Plan," episode 12, 1965–66)

"The Time Monster" (1972)

"The Time Warrior" (1973–74)

"The Invasion of Time" (1978)

"Time-Flight" (1982)

"Timelash" (1985)

"The Trial of a Time Lord" (1986)

"Time and the Rani" (1987)

"Last of the Time Lords" (2007)

"The End of Time" (2009–10)

"The Time of Angels" (2010)

"Closing Time" (2011)

"The Time of the Doctor" (2013)

Of Course, We Didn't Forget...

- **"Dimensions in Time"**: the 1993 Children in Need spectacular

- **"Time Crash"**: the 2007 Children in Need special

- **"Space/Time"**: the 2010 Comic Relief sketch

Terrible Titles of Doom

Over the years, there's been around eight hundred installments of *Doctor Who*, and counting. But not all of these episodes have been blessed with the most accurate or even very good titles. Find below a selection of the worst offenders.

"The Death of Doctor Who" (1965)

No, this wasn't a comment on the show's popularity at the time. This individual episode title from "The Chase" (back in the day when stories were made of different episode titles) actually referred to the Doctor as "Doctor Who." Sacrilege! Of course, he didn't die, thus rendering the title a lie! Watch out, however, as he is cornered by the Fungoids.

"The Deadly Assassin" (1976)

By very definition, an assassin would have to be "deadly."

"Remembrance of the Daleks" (1988)

This classic Dalek yarn has so much going for it, with lots of Dalek-on-Dalek action. But "remembrance"? Skaro's finest don't do much remembering or reminiscing in this four-parter starring Sylvester Mc-Coy as the Doctor. The title is more likely a nod to the fact that this story was broadcast during the show's 25th Anniversary and steeped in nostalgia.

"The Planet of Decision" (1965)

Another suspect episode title from "The Chase" here. The planet? Mechanus, home of the, erm, terrifying robot dustbins, the Mechonoids. The decision? Who knows? Neither the Daleks or Mechonoids were involved in any decision-making during their battle—though Ian and Barbara, two of the Doctor's original traveling companions, did decide to leave.

"The Snows of Terror" (1964)

Oooh, snow! Ooooh, scary! Mind you, having said that, the First Doctor's companions, Ian and Barbara, do pass out due to the extreme cold in this fourth episode in the epic adventure "The Keys of Marinus."

"The Invasion of Time" (1978)

Erm, Gallifrey was invaded. Don't recall time being invaded. Just sayin'.

"City of Death" (1979)

I count two deaths in the titular city, Paris. Just two. Hardly a reason to name it "City of Death." "City of a Couple of Murders" is slightly less poetic, though I'm sure writer Douglas Adams would approve.

"Survival" (1989)

Though the title is apt for the events of the final full story for the Seventh Doctor, it was rendered slightly, if not hugely, ironic by the fact that the show was soon canceled. This was the final adventure of the "classic" era and *Doctor Who* did not survive into the nineties (until it was revived, of course).

"The Doctor Dances" (2005)

Well, he did. But not until the very end! Loads of other stuff happened before that!

The United States and the Doctor

Since the show's return in 2005, *Doctor Who* has found a new source of fandom in the United States. So, unsurprisingly, this list demonstrates that the Doctor's love for the country has been more noticeable in recent years. Included here are stories set in the US of A, but not necessarily filmed there. (Fact fans will note that the computer-generated Tenth Doctor story, "Dreamland" (2009), was set in Nevada.)

"The Chase" (1965)
> This First Doctor story featured scenes at the Empire State Building in New York City (which will feature again in this list).

"The Daleks' Master Plan" (1965)
> Episode 7 (titled "The Feast of Steven") saw the First Doctor and his companions land in the middle of a Hollywood film set in the 1920s. It was broadcast on Christmas Day.

"The Gunfighters" (1966)
> Another from the original Time Lord, William Hartnell's incarnation turned up in the Wild Wild West, where he faced off against some cowboys in Tombstone, 1881.

The TV Movie (1996)
> Around thirty years later, the Seventh Doctor returned to Earth, materializing in San Francisco, only to regenerate into the Eighth.

"Dalek" (2005)
> A trip to the near future (now the past) for the Ninth Doctor, where he came face-to-face with a sole-surviving Dalek in Henry van Statten's Vault in Utah.

"Daleks in Manhattan"/"Evolution of the Daleks" (2007)
> The title says it all! And another appearance for that grand lady, the Empire State Building in New York City.

"The Stolen Earth" (2008)
> Martha Jones was now working for UNIT at their New York City headquarters when it was attacked by those dastardly Daleks.

"The End of Time" (2009–10)

Barack Obama made an "appearance" in David Tennant's finale as the Tenth Doctor, and so we were treated to scenes in the White House, in Washington, D.C.

"The Impossible Astronaut"/"Day of the Moon" (2011)

We were in Washington, D.C., again, for the Series 6 opener for the Eleventh Doctor and his chums. There were also scenes set in New York, Valley of the Gods, Area 51, Florida, and Arizona. Fact fans will note that the diner scene was filmed in a Cardiff burger joint!

"A Christmas Carol" (2010)

Very briefly, the Eleventh Doctor took Kazran and Abigail to Holly-wood (where he became engaged to actress Marilyn Monroe).

"A Town Called Mercy" (2012)

Though actually filmed in Spain (where movies such as *A Fistful of Dollars* and *The Good, the Bad, and the Ugly* were produced), this tale was set in Nevada.

"The Angels Take Manhattan" (2012)

Unsurprisingly, as the title would suggest, this story was set almost entirely in New York.

Where Are They Now?
Life after Classic *Who*

The actors who played the Doctor went on to star in many other films and shows. Let's take a look at the classic series actors and what they did after they left the TARDIS.

William Hartnell

Sadly, when the first actor to play the Doctor left the role in 1966, he was not a well man. Hartnell ventured back to television for a handful of parts, including *Doctor Who* for the multi-Doctor story "The Three Doctors" (1972), which was to be his last acting gig. He died in 1975, aged sixty-seven.

Patrick Troughton

As an actor with a wide repertoire, Troughton slipped into many roles on film and on television after he left *Doctor Who* in 1969. Notably on the big screen, he starred in *The Omen* (1976) and *Sinbad and the Eye of the Tiger* (1977), while on the small screen he guest-starred in dozens of series, but most memorably in *The Six Wives of Henry VIII* (1970) and BBC children's classic *The Box of Delights* (1984). Troughton returned another three times to the character he loved so much in "The Three Doctors" (1972), "The Five Doctors" (1983), and "The Two Doctors" (1985). He died in 1987, aged sixty-seven.

Jon Pertwee

Like Troughton, Pertwee found no trouble in finding good work on his departure, starring in a number of films, such as *Carry On Columbus* (1992), and television shows, such as *The Young Indiana Jones Chronicles* (1995) and a stint hosting murder-mystery game show *Whodunnit?* from 1974–78. But it was as Worzel Gummidge (1979) where he, arguably, found the role of a lifetime as the head-removing scarecrow. Indeed, Jon on many occasions stated he felt that was his favorite role, a part which he cherished.

Pertwee reprised his Third Doctor for "The Five Doctors" (1983); the stage show *Doctor Who: The Ultimate Adventure* (1989); the 30th Anniversary Children in Need charity special "Dimensions in Time;" and finally for the two audio stories for BBC Radio, *The Paradise of Death* (1993) and *The Ghosts of N-Space* (1996). He died in 1996, aged seventy-six.

Tom Baker

After spending seven years in the TARDIS, Baker found it slightly more difficult to find the right parts. He made a half-dozen or so movies, including 2000's *Dungeons & Dragons*, and graced television screens as Sherlock Holmes in *The Hound of the Baskervilles* (1982), *The Life and Loves of a She-Devil* (1986), *Blackadder II* (1986), and had regular roles in series such as *Medics* (1992–95), the 2000 reboot of *Randall and Hopkirk (Deceased)*, which also starred David Tennant in an episode, and, perhaps, best known for his narration on the BBC comedy *Little Britain*, which started in 2003.

Tom returned to *Doctor Who* for the 1993 charity special "Dimensions in Time," 2013's "The Day of the Doctor," and to Big Finish Productions, where he still records audio stories as the Fourth Doctor.

Peter Davison

In the UK, Peter was a well-known face on the small screen, having found fame in series like *The Tomorrow People*, *All Creatures Great and Small*, and *Sink or Swim*. Upon leaving the role as the Gallifreyan renegade in 1984, Peter was rarely off television, guest starring in dozens of shows but making a mark in *A Very Peculiar Practice* soon after *Doctor Who*, and then experienced a renaissance in the 2000s with *At Home with the Braithwaites* and *The Last Detective*. In more recent times, Davison rediscovered his love for the stage, wowing audiences in musicals such as *Chicago*, *Spamalot*, and *Legally Blonde*.

Peter returned to *Doctor Who* in "Dimensions in Time" (1993), "Time Crash" (2008), "The Five(ish) Doctors Reboot" (2013), and also for a range of Big Finish audios featuring the Fifth Doctor. He is also, now, David Tennant's father-in-law.

Colin Baker

Colin found it slightly more difficult to make his presence known in the public consciousness after Who and returned to the stage where he spent most of his time. During the 1990s and 2000s, he guest-starred in numerous series like *Casualty* and *The Bill* and reality shows in the UK such as *Come Dine With Me* and *I'm a Celebrity...Get Me Out of Here!*

Colin returned to *Doctor Who* in "Dimensions in Time" (1993), "The Five(ish) Doctors Reboot" (2013), and also for a range of Big Finish audios featuring the Sixth Doctor.

Sylvester McCoy

Likewise, Sylvester's theatrical roots saw him on stage constantly throughout the 1990s and onward in a number of varied shows, including the RSC production of King Lear in 2007 with Sir Ian McKellen (the voice of the Great Intelligence). On television, he made a handful of appearances in series like *The Bill* and *Casualty*, but more recently, McCoy starred as Radagast in The Hobbit trilogy from director, and *Doctor Who* fan, Peter Jackson.

Sylvester returned to *Doctor Who* in "Dimensions In Time" (1993), "The Five(ish) Doctors Reboot" (2013), and also for a range of Big Finish audios featuring the Seventh Doctor.

Paul McGann

Before he landed the part of the Eighth Doctor in the 1996 TV Movie, Paul McGann was acting for many years and was a very familiar face to audiences, with roles in films such as *Withnail & I* (1987), with "The Snowmen" (2012) star Richard E. Grant, and *Alien 3* (1992). After his all-too-brief one-night stand in San Francisco with the TARDIS, he graced the big screen in a number of films, including *FairyTale: A True Story* (1997), *Queen of the Damned* (2002), and *Lesbian Vampire Killers* (2009), while he consistently starred on television in dramas such as *Hornblower, Luther,* and *Jonathan Creek*. McGann is also known for his incredible narration and audiobook work, as well as for his prolific theater career.

Paul reprised his role as the Eighth Doctor in many Big Finish Production audio adventures, and on-screen in "The Night of the Doctor" (2013) and "The Five(ish) Doctors Reboot" (2013).

Where Are They Now?
Life after New *Who*

It's part two of our catch up with the actors who played the Doctor. From 2010 onward, just what have those ex-Time Lords been doing with their time?

Christopher Eccleston

Like McGann, Chris Eccleston was an established and respected actor before he took a trip in the TARDIS, and when he left, he returned to the challenging roles that had made his name. On the small screen, in 2010, he dazzled in both *Accused* (2010) and *Lennon Naked* (as John Lennon), and in the following years, in thriller series *The Shadow Line*. But the actor seemed keen to break the perception of his reputation and went stateside to appear in the television series *Heroes*, and in 2014, *The Leftovers*, while his big-screen offerings include *G.I. Joe: The Rise of Cobra* (2009) and *Thor: The Dark World* (2013).

At the time of writing, Christopher Eccleston is the only actor to have played the Doctor who has not returned to the role.

David Tennant

After *Doctor Who*, David Tennant made a strong name for himself in the world of theater; and, indeed, won high praise upon his turns in *Much Ado About Nothing* (2011) with Catherine Tate (Donna Noble) and in 2013's *Richard II*. The post-*Who* world saw him tackle the big screen in films such as *Fright Night* (2011) and *Nativity 2: Danger in the Manger* (2012), while also lending his voice to the animated flicks *How to Train Your Dragon* (2010), *The Pirates! In an Adventure with Scientists* (2012), and *Postman Pat: The Movie —You Know You're the One* (2014).

But it is in the realm of television where Tennant seems to shine best, with the fantastic crime series *Broadchurch* and its U.S. remake, *Gracepoint,* and highly acclaimed dramas like *Single Father* (2010), *United* (2011), *The Escape Artist* (2013), and *The Politician's Husband* (2013), among many, many others. Lest we forget his terrific accent, which he provided for BBC sitcoms *Twenty Twelve* (2011–12) and its sequel, *W1A* (2014), *Star Wars: The Clone Wars*, and documentaries such as *Earthflight* (2011) and *Dolphins: Spy in the Pod* (2014).

David returned to the part he made so popular and loved in the 50th Anniversary year, in "The Five(ish) Doctors Reboot" and "The Day of the Doctor."

Matt Smith

Having just left the role, Matt Smith wasted no time in securing acting parts, taking to the London stage in a musical version of *American Psycho* and then to the big screen in 2014's *Lost River* (which Smith filmed just before he filmed his 2013 *Doctor Who* finale, "The Time of the Doctor"), and signing up for the *Terminator* franchise reboot.

Peter Capaldi

At the age of fifty-five, Peter Capaldi was the equally oldest actor to play the Doctor in his initial run (matching William Hartnell). Like Eccleston, Capaldi has not returned to *Doctor Who*, mainly because he hasn't left yet. Four more years! But we're sure he'll be back for the 75th Anniversary in 2038.

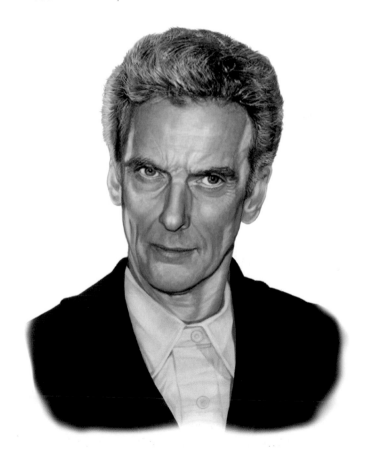

Seven Pieces Of (Murray) Gold

Since the show's return in 2005, composer Murray Gold has been the man behind *Doctor Who*'s incredible scores and themes. Murray, or MuGo, as he lets us call him, was kind enough to write down his thoughts and memories from seven of our favorite pieces of his work. Thanks, MuGo!

"The Pandorica Opens" Score (2010)

For quite a long time, the pair of episodes at the end of Series 5 were my favorites ever. We do a long suite of the music from those episodes at the live symphonic shows. I loved Toby Haynes' direction, and the storytelling, which throws images at the screen and leaves the explanations for later.

The Eleventh Doctor's Theme, "I Am the Doctor" (2010)

I have to include "I Am the Doctor" on this list just because it's so Matt Smith—silly and fun and adventurous. I know it's sort of an action theme, but it isn't very macho, because of that odd beat, and the little woodwind tune in the B section. Matt just seemed very awkward to me. So I tried to make the rhythm of his theme suitably off-beat.

When it begins playing at concerts, people's faces seem to light up a bit. Like something good has happened. And that things are going to be all right now.

"Midnight" Score (2008)

"Midnight" was like Hitchcock's *Rope*. It could have been a short play—tense and provocative, and could have been shot in one take. Probably. I liked its pessimistic view of humanity (something you didn't often find in *Doctor Who* during the Russell T. Davies years). It might seem obvious, but sometimes the obvious works in music scores. I had a piano with a delay effect so it kept repeating its notes. I colored in around it with a small band of woodwind and percussion instruments trying to capture something of the animalistic gang mentality of the humans on the bus. It was fun to go "off the hook" on that episode.

"Amy's Theme" (2010)

"Amy's Theme" was my favorite companion theme since "Rose's Theme." Amy actually has two themes, but the one I like best is the one from the second episode of Series 5 ("The Beast Below"), rather than the young Amy theme. There, I was just trying to capture a girl waiting. And hoping. And waiting.

"The Angels Take Manhattan" Score (2012)

This score was another season finale that twisted logic like an owl's head. New York is always an evocative setting musically. I think this episode and the "Daleks in Manhattan" (2007) episode were the only two that have had any saxophone in them. And those iconic shots of the hotel sign! It was sort of "Blink" in New York. I wanted to catch some of the feeling of my favorite city in the world.

Of course, it also has that heartrending ending with Matt in bits. It was painful to watch, but inevitably, when there is something painful to watch on-screen, it is quite easy to write music for it, off-screen.

"Vale Decem" from "The End of Time" Part Two (2010)

So "Vale Decem" is the song the Ood sing to the Tenth Doctor as he trudges through the snow before regenerating. Director Euros Lynn showed me the scene at my flat in New York and I started shaking. It was such a beautiful portrayal of death. David Tennant was so alone, yet urged on by these creatures who loved him.

I wanted to write a big anthem that celebrated life. I brought the choir in where the Ood lift up their arms and wrote in an instrumental lift-off where the TARDIS spins off. And a little gap for David's one devastating line, "I don't wanna go." I took a while getting the chord progression exactly right so that it unfurled slowly and climbed and climbed, but still had more to give when it seemed to have reached the top.

"Doomsday" From "Doomsday" (2006)

That scene on the beach probably defined *Doctor Who* for fans who had first met the show in 2005. Rose was such a wonderful creation. And Billie was so beautiful in the role. I was rooting around for something to take us to that beach after their separation. And I wanted it to be rock music. Like *moody* rock.

I had recorded some themes with Melanie Pappenheim for episode one of Series 1, "Rose." I was listening to them thinking I'd found one I hadn't used. Actually, the "Doomsday" theme is first heard in that first episode when Rose enters the TARDIS. But I'd forgotten that.

I just started jamming with my bass under the vocals. I pretty much played that bass line on my Fender Jazz straight out, and it totally re-harmonized the melody. A couple of edits and it was done. Then I filled in the chords on acoustic guitar and added some grungy guitar, too. Director Graeme Harper had been expecting strings, I think. But luckily the track was kept in the show. I guess it sort of captured Rose at that moment.

Murray Gold, September 2014

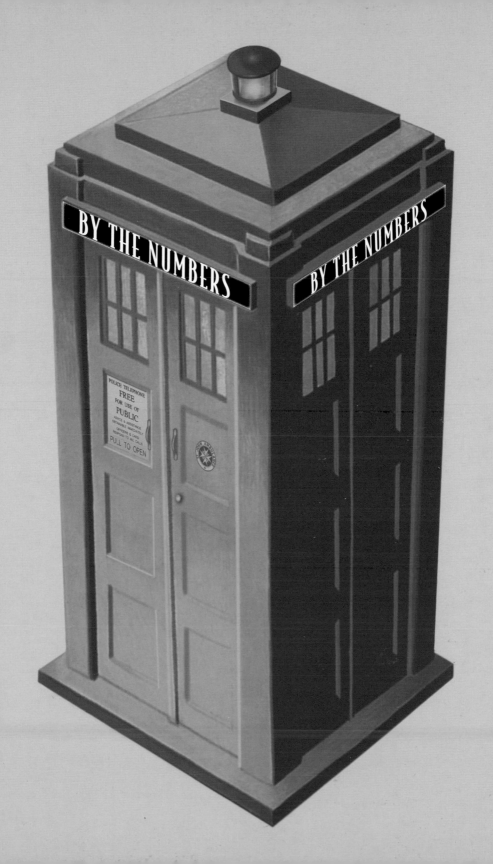

Top 20 Stories by UK Audience Ratings

People often ask what the most popular *Doctor Who* story is. Now, before you go jumping ahead to see the winner (probably already too late), there are a few things you should know. The figures here (in the millions) are consolidated from first broadcast in the UK. For stories with more than one episode, it's the average figure for all installments. All figures are from BARB (Broadcasters' Audience Research Board).

Episode	Rating	Episode	Rating
20. "Rose" (2005)	10.81	10. "The End of Time" (2009–10)	12.15
19. "The Seeds of Doom" (1976)	10.93	9. "The Deadly Assassin" (1976)	12.17
18. "The Hand of Fear" (1976)	10.95	8. "The Rescue" (1965)	12.5
17. "The Ark in Space" (1975)	11.1	7. "The Web Planet" (1965)	12.5
16. "The Time of the Doctor" (2013)	11.14	6. "The Robots of Death" (1977)	12.72
15. "The Face of Evil" (1977)	11.2	5. "The Day of the Doctor" (2013)	12.80
14. "The Romans" (1965)	11.62	4. "The Next Doctor" (2008)	13.10
13. "The Android Invasion" (1975)	11.67	3. "Voyage of the Damned" (2007)	13.31
12. "The Dalek Invasion of Earth" (2013)	11.9	2. "Destiny of the Daleks" (1979)	13.47
11. "A Christmas Carol" (2010)	12.11	1. "City of Death" (1979)	14.5

Blogtor Who's Recap

- Interestingly, or not, BBC One's main competition was on strike from early August to late October in 1979 (meaning there were only two channels to watch in the UK), which gives some context to the top two adventures.

- As a comparison, the classic series (from 1963–89) has thirteen entries while new *Who* has seven.

- And you might like to know that the Children in Need 30th Anniversary 3-D spectacular would actually be at number two, if we actually considered its existence real.

Bottom 20 Stories by UK Audience Ratings

And how about the least popular stories? As with the numbers on page 74, the figures here (in the millions) are consolidated from first broadcast in the UK. For stories with more than one episode, the average figure for all installments is represented. All figures are from BARB (Broadcasters' Audience Research Board).

Episode	Rating	Episode	Rating
20. "Greatest Show in the Galaxy" (1988–89)	5.45	10. "Survival" (1989)	4.93
19. "Remembrance of the Daleks" (1988)	5.35	9. "Paradise Towers" (1987)	4.92
18. "Delta and the Bannermen" (1987)	5.26	8. "The War Games" (1969)	4.89
17. "Full Circle" (1980)	5.25	7. "The Trial of a Time Lord" (1986)	4.80
16. "The War Machines" (1966)	5.22	6. "Meglos" (1980)	4.65
15. "State of Decay" (1980)	5.22	5. "Time and the Rani" (1987)	4.62
14. "The Leisure Hive" (1980)	5.10	4. "The Smugglers" (1966)	4.47
13. "The Happiness Patrol" (1988)	5.06	3. "The Curse of Fenric" (1989)	4.12
12. "Dragonfire" (1987)	5.06	2. "Ghost Light" (1989)	4.06
11. "The Savages" (1966)	4.97	1. "Battlefield" (1989)	3.90

Blogtor Who's Recap

- There are no entries from post-2005 *Doctor Who*.
- There is good news for Jon Pertwee and Peter Davison, as none of their stories appear here.
- Bad news for Sylvester McCoy fans, however, with all but one of his stories charting above.
- Lovers of the eighties will note that only four stories here are from another decade (all from the sixties). Tom Baker-ites may also be horrified to learn that the long-scarfed one has four stories here, while the very first adventure, "An Unearthly Child" (1963), is just outside the chart at number twenty-three.

Longest Episodes

In the olden golden days, *Doctor Who* episodes were just twenty-five minutes. Then, in the eighties, the BBC experimented with forty-five-minute installments, and then went back to twenty-five. And then they canceled it. Very occasionally, pre-2005, there were longer episodes, but upon its return in 2005, they stuck to forty-five minutes, with regular one hour-plus stories. Here are the longest single episodes of *Who* of all time!

10. "A Christmas Carol" (2010)

Running time: 62 minutes, 4 seconds

Matt Smith's first seasonal outing beats a number of the "hour" specials by clocking in a couple of extra minutes. Must've been the flying shark's fault.

9. "The Waters of Mars" (2009)

Running time: 62 minutes, 14 seconds

David Tennant's penultimate story also managed to just slightly break the hour mark by changing time in the show, too.

8. "The Eleventh Hour" (2001)

Running time: 62 minutes, 42 seconds

The debut for the Eleventh Doctor also saw the longest on-screen debut episode for a new actor in the role.

7. "Journey's End" (2008)

Running time: 63 minutes, 9 seconds

The Tennant-era gang reunion needed more time than usual to show off their skills—even longer than the Christmas specials!

6. "Voyage of the Damned" (2007)

Running time: 71 minutes, 59 seconds

An episode with pop princess Kylie Minogue and the *Titanic* had to be a beast. And to accommodate, the traditional one-hour Christmas special was lengthened accordingly by almost twelve minutes.

5. "The End of Time" Part Two (2010)
Running time: 72 minutes, 47 seconds

Fittingly, Tennant's final hurrah (well, until the next one) as the Tenth Doctor was the longest episode of his era. He would return in a longer episode a few years later in…

4. "Deep Breath" (2014)
Running time: 76 minutes, 31 seconds

Peter Capaldi's first outing as the Twelfth Doctor was a biggie and managed to beat all of his immediate predecessor's regular episodes (with only the 50th Anniversary special lasting longer).

3. "The Day of the Doctor" (2013)
Running time: 77 minutes

Though the biggest event in *Doctor Who* history, this 3-D cinema special only comes in at number three! Bested by two tales from the past…

2. TV Movie (1996)
Running time: 85 minutes, 38 seconds

For one night only, *Doctor Who* came back—with two Doctors! Sylvester McCoy and then Paul McGann entertained in a feature-length story. Sadly, it did not herald the comeback for the show.

1. "The Five Doctors" (1983)
Running time: 88 minutes, 46 seconds

The 20th Anniversary epic starring Patrick Troughton, Jon Pertwee, Tom Baker (sort of), and Peter Davison as the Doctors was rightly given a movie-esque running time. Fact fans will note that the *Special Edition* DVD version is even longer!

Longest Story Lines

Back in the classic era, story lines could last a long time. Though four-parters became the norm from the mid-seventies, there are a whole heap of *Doctor Who* adventures that defied time and entertained for hours on end. Here are the big hitters in terms of duration. (Note for time pedants: "Inferno" and "Doctor Who and the Silurians" just missed out on the top ten by a matter of minutes, despite being seven-parters like entries seven to ten.)

10. "The Daleks" (1963–64)

The Doctor's second-ever adventure, and the first featuring Skaro's finest, featured seven installments, as the First Doctor, Susan, Ian, and Barbara came to terms with the hostile planet and aliens. Clocks in at around 169 minutes.

9. "Marco Polo" (1964)

Another First Doctor seven-part story, as the original Team TARDIS pop back to 1289 to meet the titular Italian explorer. It beats the previous entry for length by three Earth minutes.

8. "The Evil of the Daleks" (1967)

More Daleks, but this time it's the Second Doctor who faces them in Patrick Troughton's first season finale. With companions Jamie Mc-Crimmon and Victoria Waterfield in tow, this also included seven episodes and sneaks ahead by just sixty seconds or so.

7. "The Ambassadors of Death" (1970)

The final of the seven-parters, and it's the Third Doctor with his only entry in the top ten (though he had two adventures just outside the list). Again, a matter of one minute separates it from the previous fellow seven-installment story.

6. "The Invasion" (1968)

Finally, an eight-part story! Troughton's Second Doctor clashes with the Cybermen in this London-based tale that lasts just over three hours.

5. "The War Games" (1969)

Troughton again, and it's the finale for the Second Doctor as he comes face-to-face with his own people for the first time in this grand epic, coming in at over four hours long.

4. The Black Guardian Trilogy (1983)

The return of the Black Guardian (more from him later) was cause for celebration, and the best way to celebrate was to take three stories and roll them into one, as the Doctor's enemy seeks revenge over three stories: "Mawdryn Undead," "Terminus," and "Enlightenment." This sequel to "The Key to Time" clocked in at five hours over twelve episodes.

3. "The Daleks' Master Plan" (1965–66)

More genuine epic Dalek fun for the First Doctor in their last adventure together, which ran for twelve installments, though really it was thirteen, as the prequel, if you like, "Mission to the Unknown," set up the story. Sadly, you can't watch this in its entirety, as episodes are missing, but if you could, you'd have to set aside over five hours to watch.

2. The Trial of a Time Lord (1985)

The second time Doctor Who attempted a season-long story saw Colin Baker's grumpy Sixth Doctor on trial by his own people, the Time Lords. Split into four parts—"The Mysterious Planet," "Mindwarp," "Terror of the Vervoids," and "The Ultimate Foe"—there were fourteen installments to savor, running to almost six hours.

1. The Key to Time (1978–79)

Encompassing six individual stories ("The Ribos Operation," "The Pirate Planet," "The Stones of Blood," "The Androids of Tara," "The Power of Kroll," and "The Armageddon Factor"), this epic twenty-six-episode adventure saw the Fourth Doctor (played by Tom Baker) and Romana (as her first incarnation, Mary Tamm) seek out the six parts of the elusive Key to Time. The assignment, given to the Time Lords by the White Guardian, lasted well over ten hours and was the first time Doctor Who had attempted a season long story arc.

Popularity of the Doctors

We've listed individual *Doctor Who* episodes and stories against what did best according to the average UK viewing public. But how do the Doctors fare against each other, according to the viewers? We've collated *every* episode and discovered what the UK average viewing figure (in millions) for each Doctor is. Let's see who wins. All figures are from BARB (Broadcasters' Audience Research Board).

Doctor		Rating
12.	Sylvester McCoy	4.8
11.	Colin Baker	6.0
10.	Patrick Troughton	7.0
9.	Peter Capaldi	7.2
8.	Peter Davison	7.5
7.	Christopher Eccleston	7.95
6.	Matt Smith	7.99
5.	Jon Pertwee	8.2
4.	David Tennant	8.36
3.	William Hartnell	8.4
2.	Paul McGann	9.08
1.	Tom Baker	9.3

And while we're talking about averages, here's a look at the top five seasons by average episode rating. As you can see, Tom Baker features heavily but is beaten by the newcomer David Tennant (specials from 2008's "The Next Doctor" until 2009's "The End of Time" Part Two) and winner Matt Smith (though it's a somewhat brief season with only two episodes, 2013's "The Day of the Doctor" and "The Time of the Doctor").

Season		Rating
5.	Season 2 (William Hartnell)	10.5
4.	Season 14 (Tom Baker)	11.1
3.	Season 17 (Tom Baker)	11.2
2.	Specials (David Tennant)	11.49
1.	2013 Specials (Matt Smith)	11.97

Percentage of the Daleks

Everyone loves a graph, right? Here you can set your eyes on pictorial proof of the popularity of Skaro's finest by Doctor. Included are appearances by the Daleks in any story (excluding episodes that use footage from previous adventures) measured up against the total for each era.

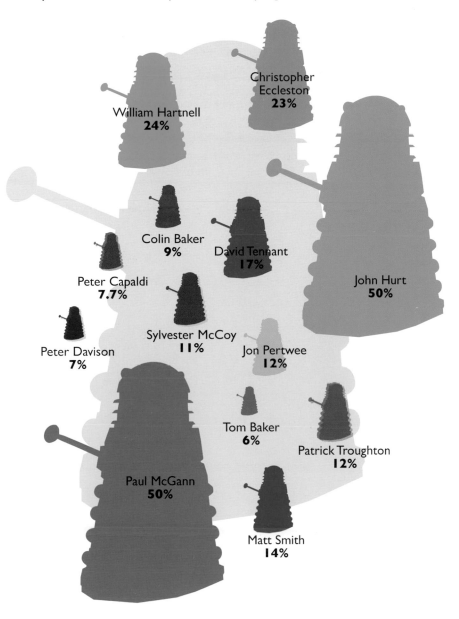

Christopher Eccleston
23%

William Hartnell
24%

Colin Baker
9%

David Tennant
17%

John Hurt
50%

Peter Capaldi
7.7%

Sylvester McCoy
11%

Jon Pertwee
12%

Peter Davison
7%

Tom Baker
6%

Patrick Troughton
12%

Paul McGann
50%

Matt Smith
14%

The Doctors' First and Last Episodes

For those of you who like numbers and stats, here's another collection to satiate your digit hunger. At the top, you'll find how the very first episodes of each Doctor began (with regard to multi-part stories, it's just the first installment) followed by each Doctor's final outing (and, again, with regard to multi-part stories, it's just the last episode we're looking at). Note that the figures here (in the millions) are consolidated from first broadcast in the UK. All figures are from BARB (Broadcasters' Audience Research Board).

Debuts

	Doctor/Episode	Rating
11.	William Hartnell ("An Unearthly Child," 1963)	4.4
10.	Sylvester McCoy ("Time and the Rani," 1987)	5.1
9.	Colin Baker ("The Twin Dilemma," 1984)	7.6
8.	Patrick Troughton ("The Power of the Daleks," 1966)	7.9
7.	Jon Pertwee ("Spearhead from Space," 1970)	8.4
6.	Paul McGann (Doctor Who, 1996)	9.08
5.	Peter Davison ("Castrovalva," 1982)	9.1
4.	David Tennant ("The Christmas Invasion," 2005)	9.84
3.	Matt Smith ("The Eleventh Hour," 2010)	10.08
2.	Tom Baker ("Robot," 1974–75)	10.8
1.	Christopher Eccleston ("Rose," 2005)	10.81

Blogtor Who's Recap

- Hartnell, Pertwee, Tennant, and Smith all managed to finish better than they began.
- Troughton, Tom Baker, and Eccleston suffered sizeable drop-offs
- Davison and Colin Baker shared a slight downturn in figures.
- McCoy finished pretty much as he began.

Finales

Doctor/Episode	Rating
11. Patrick Troughton ("The War Games," 1969)	5.0
10. Sylvester McCoy ("Survival," 1989)	5.0
9. Colin Baker ("The Trial of a Time Lord," 1986)	5.6
8. Tom Baker ("Logopolis," 1981)	6.1
7. Christopher Eccleston ("The Parting of the Ways," 2005)	6.91
6. Peter Davison ("The Caves of Androzani," 1984)	7.8
5. William Hartnell ("The Tenth Planet," 1966)	7.5
4. Jon Pertwee ("Planet of the Spiders," 1974)	8.9
3. Paul McGann (*Doctor Who*, 1996)	9.08
2. Matt Smith ("The Time of the Doctor," 2013)	11.14
1. David Tennant ("The End of Time," 2009–10)	12.27

The Doctors' Highs and Lows

Here are the best- and worst-performing single episodes for each Doctor. The figures here (in the millions) are consolidated from first broadcast in the UK. All figures are from BARB (Broadcasters' Audience Research Board).

Highs		
11.	Sylvester McCoy ("The Greatest Show in the Galaxy," episode 4, 1988–89)	6.6
10.	Colin Baker ("Attack of the Cybermen," episode 1, 1985)	8.9
9.	Patrick Troughton ("The Krotons," episode 1, 1968–69)	9.0
8.	Paul McGann (Doctor Who, 1996)	9.08
7.	Peter Davison ("Castrovalva," episode 4, 1982)	10.4
6.	Christopher Eccleston ("Rose," 2005)	10.81
5.	Jon Pertwee ("The Three Doctors," episode 4, 1972–73)	11.9
4.	Matt Smith ("The Day of the Doctor," 2013)	12.8
3.	David Tennant ("Voyage of the Damned," 2007)	13.31
2.	William Hartnell ("The Web Planet," episode 1, 1965)	13.5
1.	Tom Baker ("City of Death," episode 4, 1979)	16.10
Lows		
11.	Paul McGann (Doctor Who, 1996)	9.08
10.	Christopher Eccleston ("Bad Wolf," 2005)	6.81
9.	Matt Smith ("The Lodger," 2010)	6.44
8.	David Tennant ("The Satan Pit," 2006)	6.08
7.	Peter Davison ("Frontios," episode 4, 1984)	5.6
6.	Jon Pertwee ("Inferno," episode 3, 1970)	4.8
5.	William Hartnell ("The Smugglers," episode 3, 1966)	4.2
4.	Tom Baker ("Full Circle," episode 2, 1980)	3.7
3.	Colin Baker ("The Trial of a Time Lord," episode 4, 1986)	3.7
2.	Patrick Troughton ("The War Games," episode 8, 1969)	3.5
1.	Sylvester McCoy ("Battlefield," episode 1, 1989)	3.1

The Time of the Doctors

Here we take a look at a graph showing the screen times of each of the actors who have played the Time Lord (including the 1960s movie incarnation). We've also taken into account the various returns in all the multi-Doctor stories.

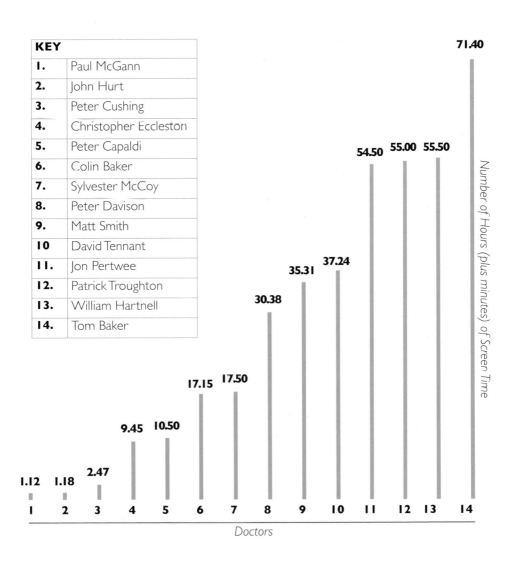

KEY	
1.	Paul McGann
2.	John Hurt
3.	Peter Cushing
4.	Christopher Eccleston
5.	Peter Capaldi
6.	Colin Baker
7.	Sylvester McCoy
8.	Peter Davison
9.	Matt Smith
10	David Tennant
11.	Jon Pertwee
12.	Patrick Troughton
13.	William Hartnell
14.	Tom Baker

Number of Hours (plus minutes) of Screen Time

Doctors

1.12   1.18   2.47   9.45   10.50   17.15   17.50   30.38   35.31   37.24   54.50   55.00   55.50   71.40

1   2   3   4   5   6   7   8   9   10   11   12   13   14

The Time of the Writers

Doctor Who has been blessed with many amazing and talented writers since its start in 1963. And many have returned time and again to pen new adventures for the Gallifreyan. Here's a chart depicting those who have written the most stories for the Doctor. Please note: this list pertains to televised *Doctor Who* episodes (no mini-episodes, DVD extras, or anything of that nature).

Writer		Number of Stories
10.	Terrance Dicks	6
8.	Malcolm Hulke	7
8.	Mark Gatiss	7
6.	David Whitaker	8
6.	Dave Martin	8
5.	Bob Baker	9
4.	Terry Nation	11
3.	Robert Holmes	18
2.	Russell T. Davies	25
1.	Steven Moffat	28

The Age of the Doctors

Here's one for age fans. Below you'll find a table that illustrates the various ages involved in playing the Doctor. In it you'll see the ages of the actors when they first appeared on television as the Doctor (though some actors were a year younger when they actually started filming) and the ages they were in their last appearances (1972–73's "The Three Doctors" for Hartnell, 1983's "The Five Doctors" for Pertwee, etc.).

Doctor	First	Last	Doctor	First	Last
William Hartnell	55	64*	Paul McGann	36	54
Patrick Troughton	46	64	John Hurt	73	73
Jon Pertwee	50	64	Christopher Eccleston	41	41
Tom Baker	40	79	David Tennant	34	42
Peter Davison	29**	56	Matt Smith	27	31
Colin Baker	40	43	Peter Capaldi	55	?
Sylvester McCoy	44	52			

* Turned 65 during the airing of the four-parter "The Three Doctors" (1972–73).
** Turned 30 by the time his first full story, "Castrovalva" (1982), aired.

The Height of the Doctors

Unlike James Bond, there's no call to have the Doctor be a six-foot-plus Adonis (what about Daniel Craig?), so there have been varying heights of actors who've played the Time Lord, starting with the hobbity McCoy and finishing with the veritable giants of Pertwee and Baker.

(For those curious, the average is 5'9".)

6'0"
Colin Baker

6'0"
Christopher
Eccleston

6'0"
Peter
Capaldi

6'0"
Peter
Davison

6'0"
David
Tennant

6'2"
Jon
Pertwee

6'2"
Tom Baker

5 Times When the Doctor Changed History

The First Doctor once said, "You can't rewrite history—not one line!"—that was in "The Aztecs" (1964), fact fans! And yet he has done so a number of times. Or was that how it was always meant to be…? We'll let you decide, but here are five stories when the Doctor changed or directly influenced real life human history.

"The Romans" (1965)

Due to some errant spectacle holding (which led to plans of Rome going up in flames), the First Doctor gave the idea of burning down Rome to Roman Emperor Nero. The fire ravaged Rome in 64 AD. Some years later, the Tenth Doctor later told Donna Noble he was not responsible for Rome burning (or, in his words, "not exactly"). Speaking of which…

"The Fires of Pompeii" (2008)

Tricky one, this. Was Vesuvius meant to explode or not? Either way, the Doctor was directly involved when he and Donna took a trip to Pompeii in 79 AD. The Pyroviles had their eyes set on conquering the world; though the Time Lord averted this, he still caused the volcano to erupt so disastrously.

"Earthshock" (1982)

Poor Adric. The Fifth Doctor's companion came to a rather unfortunate end when he tried to stop a spaceship crashing into Earth (due to those pesky, yet excellent, Cybermen). Thankfully, for the human race, the smash resulted in the end of the dinosaurs.

"The Shakespeare Code" (2007)

When the Tenth Doctor and Martha Jones took a trip back in time to visit William Shakespeare (or Bill, as some call him), they inadvertently inspired the author to coin the phrase, "To be or not to be," (from *Hamlet*) while introducing the familiar "Author, Author!" to audiences. "Do people shout that? Do they shout Author?" asked Martha, to which her buddy Ten replied, "Well, they do now!"

Similarly, Donna Noble would provide Agatha Christie with the title *Murder on the Orient Express* in "The Unicorn and the Wasp" (2008).

"The Visitation" (1982)

Perhaps the most obvious, not to mention devastating, influence the Doctor has shown was in the creation of The Great Fire of London back in 1666. The blaze began after the Fifth Doctor had a run-in with those nasty aliens the Terileptils (who had already destroyed the Time Lord's old friend, the Sonic Screwdriver). Their leader's weapon began to overheat and the resulting detonation started the fire that caused so much havoc to the city. And all because the Doctor was looking for Heathrow!

6 Times the Doctor Predicted the Future

Given that *Doctor Who* is a show all about time travel (well, some of the time), it's not so surprising when it predicts the future. What is surprising is when *Doctor Who* predicts the future correctly. Here are some of those rare times.

"The Invasion" (1968)—Automated Telephones

This Second Doctor adventure, featuring an attack on Earth by the Cybermen, saw the bane of many people's existence in modern times—an automated telephone service. Things don't go well when communicating with one of the International Electromatic Company's machines, leaving it to companion, and astrophysicist, Zoe Heriot to sum it up rather pithily: "Now listen to me, you stupid, primitive machine. I asked a perfectly simple question, and I expect an answer." You go, girl!

"The Dæmons" (1971)—BBC Three

Some thirty-two years before its actual appearance on UK small televisions, this Third Doctor story saw BBC Three covering an archaeological dig at Devil's Hump in deepest, darkest England. Sadly for the channel—which gave us the wonderful "making of" series *Doctor Who Confidential*—its days are numbered, with BBC Three heading online.

"Terror of the Zygons" (1975)—Female Prime Minister for the UK

Some eerie prophesizing was going on in this Fourth Doctor tale featuring those sucker shapeshifters. Upon receiving a call from the Prime Minister, the Brigadier states, "Oh, absolutely understood, madame." It would be just four years later when Margaret Thatcher would be voted in to that very office, creating more havoc than even the Sakarasen!

"Vengeance on Varos" (1985)—Reality Television

Big Brother? *Survivor*? Pah, you've got nothing on *Doctor Who*. (Well, we knew that already, didn't we?) The planet Varos was keen on getting viewers to vote on whom to torture and kill in their interactive television show. While the planet Earth hasn't quite gotten around to being so extreme, we can guess it's only a matter of time.

"Battlefield" (1989)—Five Pound Coin

Slight cheat here as the five pound coin has never been in wide circulation, but less than a year after this Seventh Doctor story (set in the late 1990s) hit screens, the very same currency was released as a commemorative coin in the UK.

"Fear Her" (2006)—The Doctor Carries the Olympic Torch

Ok, this one is also slightly tenuous. *But*, the Tenth Doctor did carry the Olympic torch in the suburban tale from David Tennant's first series as the Time Lord—just as Matt Smith did shortly before the games began in London in 2012.

15 Things People Did In "The Wilderness Years"

For whatever reasons they saw fit, the BBC canned *Doctor Who* after its 26th season in 1989, signing off with Sylvester McCoy as the Seventh Doctor. The show came back briefly in 1996 with the brilliant Paul McGann and then tooled off into the sunset until its bold return with Christopher Eccleston in 2005. But what did we, in the UK, do in those fifteen or so years when there was no new *Who* on the telly? You're about to find out—so, starting from 1990…

1. Mourned the loss of Doctor Who…

2. Wrote letters to the BBC furiously asking for its return.

3. Got excited for new Seventh Doctor stories in a series of books called *The New Adventures* from Virgin Publishing!

4. "Celebrated" the 30th Anniversary with the 3-D special, "Dimensions in Time."

5. Wrote letters to the BBC furiously asking why they made "Dimensions in Time."

6. Set expectations to "cautiously optimistic" when it was rumored Steven Spielberg might be bringing Who back.

7. Got excited for the 1996 Paul McGann TV Movie! Bought the books, the magazines, the VHS, and then lamented the fact that he was gone so soon as the Eighth Doctor.

8. Mourned the loss of *Doctor Who*…again.

9. Wrote letters to the BBC furiously asking for its return. Again.

10. Started to collect the stories we already owned on the new format, DVD, and then started selling our VHS collections on eBay.

11. Got excited in 2001 when Big Finish Productions started to release audio dramas featuring the Doctors!

12. Started to come to terms with the fact that Doctor Who may be consigned to online animated adventures.

13. Got slightly baffled by the appearance of "Scream of the Shalka" (2003), starring Richard E. Grant as the Doctor, on the BBC website (now available on DVD).

14. Accepted that Doctor Who was never going to return to television.

15. Got excited for its return with Christopher Eccleston and Billie Piper!

Actors Who Have Been in Both *Star Wars* and *Doctor Who*

In some places in the world, *Star Wars* is even bigger than *Doctor Who*—crazy, I know! Interestingly, there have been a great number of actors who've been familiar with both sonics and lightsabers over the years. Here are some of the more memorable ones.

Silas Carson

Silas Carson is in the enviable position of appearing as a number of characters in the *Star Wars* prequel universe (Nute Gunray, Ki-Adi-Mundi, Lott Dodd, and a Republic Cruiser Pilot), but in the Whoniverse, he's in the even more impressive situation of voicing the Ood. The bald aliens with their brains in their hands (sometimes) first appeared in "The Impossible Planet" (2006) and proved such a hit, they returned just two years later for "Planet of the Ood" (2008), "The Waters of Mars" (2009), and "The End of Time" (2009–10), and then again for "The Doctor's Wife" (2010), all voiced by Mr. Carson. A most memorable *Doctor Who* alien and *Star Wars* Jedi.

Julian Glover

Shakespearian actor Julian Glover first appeared in *Doctor Who* in the William Hartnell era in the slightly missing story "The Crusade" (1964). He would return in the most-watched *Who* story ever, "City of Death" (1979), as one of the show's most memorable villains: Scaroth, the one-eyed Jaggaroth. And then Glover made the step up, or down, depending on how you view it, into Darth Vader's Imperial Army in the 1980 classic, *The Empire Strikes Back*, as General Veers.

Michael Sheard

Similarly, Michael Sheard had made many great performances over the years in *Doctor Who*. Just check out "The Ark" (1966), "The Mind of Evil" (1971), "Pyramids of Mars" (1975), and "The Invisible Enemy" (1977) before he, like Julian Glover above, made the jump to the dark side and starred in *The Empire Strikes Back* as Admiral Ozzel. His brevity in the *Star Wars* universe, dying at the hands of Darth Vader, meant a return to *Who* as the Portreve in Peter Davison's first story, "Castrovalva" (1982) and then in the 25th Anniversary classic with Sylvester McCoy, "Remembrance of the Daleks" (1988).

David Prowse

The big man himself, Darth Vader, popped up in *Doctor Who* (in the 1972 Jon Pertwee story "The Time Monster") long before David Prowse donned the black cape and breathing mask in the George Lucas space opera. And, just like his Sith-based performance, David Prowse played the Minotaur in his typically gargantuan style.

Jeremy Bulloch

Speaking of bad boys, the man behind Boba Fett was there in the early days of *Doctor Who*. Jeremy Bulloch graced the screen with Hartnell in the 1965 tale "The Space Museum" as Tor, and then more memorably as Hal the Archer in the 1974 classic "The Time Warrior" (which also introduced the world to Sarah Jane Smith). It would be a few years until his most famous role as the Mandolarian warrior, making him a legend to *Who* and *Star Wars* fans worldwide.

Peter Cushing

Darth Vader's sidekick, Tarkin, was known to *Doctor Who* fans, or the movie theater–visiting ones at least, as the character "Dr. Who" in the two wonderful cinematic treats *Dr. Who and the Daleks* (1965) and *Daleks' Invasion Earth 2150 AD* (1966). Peter Cushing starred as the titular Earth-bound scientist who built a time machine in his garden in 1964 and 1965 but, sadly, didn't return for more Dalek-based fun.

Warwick Davis

Warwick Davis got his big break as an eight-year-old in one of the biggest movies of the eighties, *Return of the Jedi*. Davis impressed as loveable Ewok Wicket, flirting with the even more loveable Princess Leia and helping the Rebels defeat the Empire. But it would be thirty years later before he graced the world of *Doctor Who* in the Neil Gaiman Cybermen episode, "Nightmare in Silver" (2013), as Porridge (and also Emperor of the Universe). And just as adorable.

Brian Blessed

In his home country, the UK, Brian Blessed is regarded somewhat as a national treasure with his shouting, loud-voiced antics, and more shouting. Familiar to many for bellowing "Gordon's alive!" in the 1980 version of Flash Gordon, Big Brian (and he is BIG) made for an odd ally to the Sixth Doctor in "The Trial of a Time Lord" (1986). Bizarrely, his character, King Ycarnos, ended up marrying American companion Peri. But if you thought that was bizarre, then do take a cursory glance at his performance as leader of the Gungans, Boss Nass, in *Star Wars: Episode I*. Well, take a listen anyway. The blustering, spitting alien was voiced by Brian, while his physical appearance was computer-generated.

Lindsay Duncan

Like Blessed above, Lindsay Duncan's voice was also heard in *The Phantom Menace* as shiny silver protocol droid TC-14 (a blink-and-you'll-miss-it turn at the start of the film). She was looking after Jedi Qui Gon Jinn and Obi-Wan Kenobi (rather poorly, it should be said) shortly before they found the young Darth Vader, Anakin Skywalker. The British actress would be more recognizable as the formidable Adelaide Brooke in the 2009 adventure for the Tenth Doctor "The Waters of Mars."

Celia Imrie

A fellow British actress, Celia Imrie has the esteemed position of being the first female pilot in the *Star Wars* movie franchise (Fighter Pilot Bravo 5 in *The Phantom Menace*). A small role there, but in the world of *Who*, she vamped it up nicely as the child taken away from her parents and turned into a nasty piece of work by The Great Intelligence in "The Bells of Saint John" (2013).

David Tennant

Yup, you read correctly. David Tennant, for many fans *the* Doctor, voiced the Jedi architect droid Professor Huyang in two episodes of the *Star Wars* animated series *The Clone Wars* in 2012. Fact fans will note that the Scottish Aptor won an Emmy for his performance. (See also: Simon Pegg, the Editor in 2005's "The Long Game" (2005), who voiced bounty hunter Dengar the same year.)

Burnell Tucker

Though that may sound like a character name, that is, in fact, his real name. Burnell Tucker performed the important role of Other Rebel Officer in *The Empire Strikes Back*, and in 2012's "The Angels Take Manhattan," he played the older version of Sam Garner.

Garrick Hagon

Garrick Hagon has graced *Doctor Who* twice, and in between each appearance, he managed a memorable, if slightly edited, role as Luke Skywalker's best bud, Biggs Darklighter, in *A New Hope*. He came to a sad end at the hands of the Empire, but in *Doctor Who*, he flourished as Ky in the 1972 Jon Pertwee adventure "The Mutants" and as Abrahams in the more recent 2012 western, "A Town Called Mercy," where he could be seen measuring up the Eleventh Doctor for a coffin.

Milton Johns

Like a number of actors in "classic" *Doctor Who*, Milton Johns turned up
in a few stories over the years. His first *Who* action came in the Patrick
Troughton story "The Enemy of the World" (1968) as Benik, and then
he returned for his most memorable role as Guy Crayford in "The
Android Invasion" (1975), before finishing his time on the show in
another Tom Baker tale as a fellow Time Lord in "The Invasion of Time"
(1978). Just a couple of years later, he would play an Imperial Officer
in *The Empire Strikes Back* (alongside many *Who* alumni). Interestingly,
Milton appears in two scenes: one where his own voice was used and
another where he was overdubbed.

Alan Roscoe

Maybe not a familiar name, or even face, but Alan Roscoe has appeared in more episodes and as more characters than anyone else here on this list! First up, in the *Star Wars* films, he played Neimodian Daultay Dofine, Jedi Plo Koon, and Jabba's BFF, Bib Fortuna, in *The Phantom Menace*, and Neimodian Lott Dod in *Attack of the Clones*. In the Whoniverse, deep breath, he was busy in 2005 playing an Auton in "Rose"; a Forest of Cheem Tree in "The End of the World"; a Slitheen in "Aliens of London"/"World War Three" and "Boom Town"; robots Trine-E and the Anne Droid in "Bad Wolf"/"Parting of the Ways"; and then more recognizably (showing his face anyway) as the doomed member of Bowie Base One, Andy Stone, in "The Waters of Mars" (2009). Alan, we salute you!

Honorable Mention

- **Hugh Quarshie** (Captain Panaka in *The Phantom Menace* and Solomon in 2007's "Daleks in Manhattan"/"Evolution of the Daleks")

- **Don Henderson** (General Tagge in *A New Hope* and Gavrok in 1987's "Delta and the Bannermen")

- **Leslie Schofield** (an Imperial Commander in *A New Hope* and Leroy in 1969's "The War Games" and Calib in 1977's "The Face of Evil")

- **John Hollis** (Lobot in *The Empire Strikes Back* and Sondergaard in 1972's "The Mutants")

- **Steve Speirs** (voice of Captain Tarpals in *The Phantom Menace* and Strickland the Slitheen in 2005's "Aliens of London"/"World War Three")

- **Ayesha Dharker** (Queen Jamillia in *Attack of the Clones* and Solana Mercurio in 2008's "Planet of the Ood")

- **Shane Rimmer** (an unnamed engineer in *A New Hope* and Seth Harper in 1966's "The Gunfighters")

Agatha Christie Stories Referenced in "The Unicorn and the Wasp"

Gareth Roberts' brilliant 2008 story featuring the famous author included a number of direct references and mentions to her works (short stories and novels). See if you spotted them all (in chronological appearance in the episode).

Donna Noble: "Hold on, the body in the library?"
—*The Body in the Library*

Donna Noble: "Next thing you know, you'll be telling me it's like *Murder on the Orient Express*, and they all did it."
—*Murder on the Orient Express*

Agatha Christie: "No alibis for any of them. The secret adversary remains hidden."
—*The Secret Adversary*

The Doctor: "What's that first letter? N or M?"
—*N or M?*

Agatha Christie: "We're still no further forward. Our nemesis remains at large."
—*Nemesis* (Fact Fans will note that "Nemesis" was the title of the *Doctor Who Confidential* episode that accompanies this story.)

Mrs. Hart: "A murder? That's put the cat among the pigeons and no mistake."
—*Cat Among the Pigeons*

Miss Chandrakala: "A dead man's folly, nothing more."
—*Dead Man's Folly*

Agatha Christie: "It can't be a monster. It's a trick. They do it with mirrors."
—*They Do It with Mirrors*

Lady Eddison: "She never found me. She had an appointment with death instead."
—*Appointment with Death*

Colonel Hugh Curbishley: "Heavens' sake, cards on the table, woman."
—*Cards on the Table*

Agatha Christie: "Bitter almonds. It's cyanide, sparkling cyanide."
—*Sparkling Cyanide*

The Doctor: "I've called you here on this endless night, because we have a murderer in our midst."
—*Endless Night*

Agatha Christie: "This is a crooked house. A house of secrets."
—*Crooked House*

Lady Eddison: "The river Jumna rose up and broke its banks. He was taken at the flood."
—*Taken at the Flood*

The Doctor: "The moving finger points at you, Lady Eddison."
—*The Moving Finger*

Agatha Christie: "Death comes as the end, and justice is served."
—*Death Comes as the End*

Close, but not quite there…

Professor Peach: "It's unbelievable. But why didn't they ask? Heavens!"
—*Why Didn't They Ask Evans?*

The Doctor: "Murder at the vicar's rage. Needs a bit of work."
—*The Murder at the Vicarage*

Of Course, We Didn't Forget...

- **Yellow Iris:** a vase of the flowers is seen on a table.
- **Death in the Clouds** and **The Murder of Roger Ackroyd:** editions of both of these books are seen.
- **The Man in the Brown Suit:** as worn by Tennant himself throughout the episode!

DECEMBER 3rd 1926

Detective
Mystery Magazine

1/-
NET

THE UNICORN and the WASP

Cameos

Though the Doctor has met many different sorts of people in the universe, occasionally he meets someone that us mere mortals on Earth actually recognize. Check out some of the British people and personalities who have come into contact with the Time Lord's adventures.

McFly

Still with us, incredibly, despite their questionable musical ability, the UK beat combo lent their support to the Harold "Harry" Saxon campaign on UK television along with some other "celebs" of the day.

Lord Alan Sugar

Businessman Big Al, as no one calls him, utilized the cubes sent to Earth by the Shakri by featuring the alien objects on his version of the Donald Trump reality television show, "The Apprentice." Once a Sir, now a Lord, the Sugarman is more akin to one of the many alien monsters the Doctor has faced rather than a companion.

Courtney Pine

While relaxing with his chum Ace, the Seventh Doctor revealed he was quite the fan of jazz saxophonist Courtney Pine. The couple enjoyed his soothing sounds shortly before uncovering a dastardly Cybermen plot. Ace, clearly a fan, stated, "I could listen to him all afternoon," before getting an autograph from the man. The Gallifreyan also chipped in with his approval, claiming it was his "favorite kind of jazz."

Andrew Marr

Numerous news anchors have crossed paths with the Doctor over the years (much-loved Kenneth Kendall of BBC One being the first), and Mr. Marr is part of that esteemed and much-lauded list. He reported for the BBC just outside 10 Downing Street as, unbeknownst to the journalist, the Slitheen family was infiltrating the UK government.

Professor Brian Cox

The Prof, as he likes to be known, supported the theory that the objects involved in the "slow invasion of the cubes" (instigated by the Shakri) could have been extraterrestrial in origin—though he wasn't convinced. Pity his path didn't cross with the Eleventh Doctor; he'd have made a most excellent TARDIS companion!

Sharon Osbourne

The wife of Ozzy Osbourne didn't come into direct contact with the Doctor, but she did support the alter ego of his fellow Gallifreyan, the Master. Shazza publicly championed Harold Saxon in his bid to become the UK Prime Minister—he certainly did have the "X Factor" when it came to world domination.

Sir Patrick Moore

Sadly no longer with us, Sir Patrick helped out the Eleventh Doctor via an Internet conference call with other Earth scientists during an attack by the Atraxi on the planet. A "devil" with the ladies, according to the Time Lord, the well-known British astronomer was also name-checked by Rose Tyler to the Ninth Doctor when the Slitheen attempted to destroy all life on Earth.

Professor Richard Dawkins

When the Daleks moved Earth, along with twenty-six other planets, to the Medusa Cascade, this God-loving scientist appeared on the television show *Universally Speaking*. Combating the viewpoint that some humans obviously didn't believe Earth had moved, the professor stated, "The planets didn't come to us, we came to them!" Although unseen, his wife bears a striking resemblance to Time Lady Romana, in her second incarnation.

The Beatles

The biggest of the bestest, the poppermost of the toppermost, the sounds of The Beatles filled the TARDIS as the First Doctor proudly displayed his Time-Space Visualiser to companions Vicki, Ian, and Barbara. Oddly, Ian seemed to be all too familiar with the track "Ticket to Ride" despite having left Earth more than a year before its single release.

Bonus! Meredith Vieira

Speaking of news people, Meredith Viera is a special entry, being the only American on the list. Even more special was the fact that she reported in an alternate time line where the Earth was stuck in one moment in time. She was good, but she was no Trinity Wells.

Pop Songs in Classic *Who*

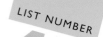

Everyone loves a good song, no more so than the makers of *Doctor Who*. Please find a rather complete list of pop songs (with the odd rock one thrown in for good measure) used from 1963 up until 1989. This would make quite a playlist!

"Blue Suede Shoes," in "Revelation of the Daleks" (1985)*

"Do You Want to Know a Secret?," the Beatles, in "Remembrance of the Daleks" (1988)

"Fire," Jimi Hendrix, in "Revelation of the Daleks" (1985)

"Good Vibrations," in "Revelation of the Daleks" (1985)*

"Hound Dog," in "Revelation of the Daleks" (1985)*

"Nobody Knows the Trouble I've Seen," the Seekers, in "The Evil of the Daleks" (1967)

"Oh Well," Fleetwood Mac, in "Spearhead from Space" (1970)

"Paperback Writer," the Beatles, in "The Evil of the Daleks" (1967)

"Rock Around the Clock," in "Delta and the Bannermen" (1987)*

"A Taste of Honey," the Beatles, in "Remembrance of the Daleks" (1988)

"Ticket to Ride," the Beatles, in "The Chase" (1965)

"That'll Be the Day," in "Delta and the Bannermen" (1987)*

"A Whiter Shade of Pale," Procol Harum, in "Revelation of the Daleks" (1985)

"Why Do Fools Fall in Love?" in "Delta and the Bannermen" (1987)*

(Note for pedants: some tracks were removed from the DVD releases for copyright issues.)

*Not original artist's recording

Pop Songs in New *Who*

Opposite, we looked at pop and rock songs in the classic era of *Doctor Who*. Now here's the post-2005 list. Within ten years, there's double the use of Earth songs!

"Another Brick in the Wall (Part 2)," Pink Floyd in "The Caretaker" (2014)

"The Birdie Song," the Tweets, in "The Power of Three" (2012)

"Bohemian Rhapsody," Queen (sung by cast), in "Turn Left" (2008)

"Brand New Key," Melanie (performed by LINDA), in "Love & Monsters" (2006)

"Chances," Athlete, in "Vincent and the Doctor" (2010)

"Crazy Little Thing Called Love," Queen, in "The Big Bang" (2010)

"Daniel," Elton John, in "Love & Monsters" (2006)

"Do It Do It Again," Rafaella Carra, in "Midnight" (2008)

"Don't Bring Me Down," Electric Light Orchestra (performed by LINDA), in "Love & Monsters" (2006)

"Don't Mug Yourself," The Streets, in "Father's Day" (2005)

"Don't Stop Me Now," Queen, in "Mummy on the Orient Express" (2014)

"An Englishman in New York," Sting, in "The Angels Take Manhattan" (2012)

"Feel the Love," Rudimental featuring John Newman, in "Asylum of the Daleks" (2012)

"Fire Woman," The Cult, in "Journey to the Centre of the TARDIS" (2013)

"Ghost Town," The Specials, in "The Rings of Akhaten" (2013)

"Hey Mickey," Toni Basil, in "Death in Heaven" (2014)

"Hit Me with Your Rhythm Stick," Ian Dury & the Blockheads, in "Tooth and Claw" (2006)

"Hungry Like the Wolf," Duran Duran, in "Cold War" (2013)

"I Can't Decide," Scissor Sisters, in "Last of the Time Lords" (2007)

"The Lion Sleeps Tonight," Tight Fit, in "Rise of the Cybermen" (2006)

"Love Will Tear Us Apart," Joy Division, in "School Reunion" (2006)

"Macarena," Los del Río, in "The Girl Who Waited" (2011)

"Merry Xmas Everybody," Slade, in "The Christmas Invasion" (2005), "The Runaway Bride" (2006) and "Turn Left" (2008)

"Mr. Blue Sky," Electric Light Orchestra, in "Love & Monsters" (2006)

"Never Can Say Goodbye," The Communards, in "Father's Day" (2005)

"Never Gonna Give You Up," Rick Astley, in "Father's Day" (2005)

"Rolling in the Deep," Adele, in "The Impossible Astronaut" (2011)

"Starman," David Bowie, in "Aliens of London" (2005)

"Supermassive Black Hole," Muse, in "The Rebel Flesh" (2011)

"Tainted Love," Soft Cell, in "The End of the World" (2005)

"Titanium," David Guetta featuring Sia, in "The Power of Three" (2012)

"Toxic," Britney Spears in, "The End of the World" (2005)

"Twenty Four Hours from Tulsa," Gene Pitney, in "Partners in Crime" (2008)

"Vienna," Ultravox, in "Cold War" (2013)

"Voodoo Child," Rogue Traders, in "The Sound of Drums" (2007)

"You Don't Have to Say You Love Me," Dusty Springfield, in "The Rebel Flesh" (2011)

"You Give Me Something," James Morrison, in "The Big Bang" (2010)

Starman waiting in the Sky

Films That Featured
Doctor Who Stars

Occasionally, when you're sitting at your local movie theater, you might notice a familiar face from the world of *Doctor Who* popping up in the most unexpected of places. And we don't mean the concession stands. Below you'll find some movies that you may well be surprised to discover casted actors from *Doctor Who*!

Inception

Christopher Nolan's dreamy sci-fi epic may seem a world away from *Doctor Who*, but you'll find two names familiar to fans: Talulah Riley, the lovely and doomed Miss Evangelista in "Silence in the Library"/"Forest of the Dead (2008)," plays the interestingly named "Blonde," while Earl Cameron, astronaut Glyn Williams in William Hartnell's finale, "The Tenth Planet (1966)," portrays the equally interestingly named "Elderly Bald Man."

Captain America

Back in 2011, the first of the new Marvel Captain America films was released. Titled *The First Avenger*, this flick had a number of big names from *Who*, and none more so than companion Clara Oswald herself, played by Jenna Coleman (back when she used Louise as a middle name). Playing Connie, girlfriend of Steve Rogers' friend Bucky, it's a blink-and-you'll-miss-it performance. But don't dismay, as there's David Bradley's Solomon from "Dinosaurs on a Spaceship" (2012) and Michael Brandon's UNIT General Sanchez from "The Stolen Earth" (2008) to check out, too. The sequel, *The Winter Soldier* (2014), saw The Dream Lord (Toby Jones in 2010's "Amy's Choice") pop up. Jones can also be seen in *The Hunger Games*.

X-Men

Sticking with superhero flicks, the X-Men series has thrown up a number of big names from *Doctor Who*. The voice of the Great Intelligence, Sir Ian McKellen, is, of course, well known for his role as Magneto in the franchise, while Brian Cox voiced the Ood in David Tennant's finale, "The End of Time" (2009), and played nasty military man William Stryker in *X2* (2003). In the X-Men spin-off *The Wolverine* (2009), Australian actor Peter O'Brien (Bowie Base One's second in command, Ed Gold, in 2009's "The Waters of Mars") starred as Wolverine's stepdad, John Howlett. A few years later, the series got a reboot of sorts, with *X-Men: First Class*, which saw a plethora of *Who* names, including Laurence Belcher, who plays the very young Charles Xavier and the young Kazran Sardick in Matt Smith's first special, "A Christmas Carol" (2010); Corey Johnson, the infamous Henry van Statten in 2005's "Dalek," plays a Chief Warden; and Vincent van Gogh himself, Tony Curran, who plays an unnamed agent. Completists and fact fans will note that Jason Flemyng's (teleporting mutant Azazel) dad, Gordon Flemyng, directed the two Peter Cushing Dalek movies in the sixties.

Les Misérables

Everyone loves a cheery sing-song, don't they? Well, this is certainly a sing-song at any rate, but it also features a gang of surprising *Who* faces. For example, who would have thought that Davros would make a tasty baritone? Skaro's finest, played by Julian Bleach, makes an appearance, as does Simon Fisher-Becker (the Eleventh Doctor's chum Dorium Maldovar); Daniel Evans (Danny Llewellyn, killed by a Sycorax whip in "The Christmas Invasion" (2005); and Adrian Scarborough (Kahler-Jex from 2012's "A Town Called Mercy").

The Twilight Saga

Yup, even the teen series *Twilight* has space for *Doctor Who*. Scooti from "The Impossible Planet"/"The Satan Pit" (2006), actress MyAnna Buring, stars as Tanya Denali in the "saga," whilst the voice of House in "The Doctor's Wife" (2011), Welsh actor Michael Sheen, has numerous appearances throughout the franchise as Aro, one of the leaders of the Volturi.

The Iron Lady

Maybe not that surprising to find some *Who* people here, given that it's about Margaret Thatcher and set in the UK (and not, in fact, a spin-off from *Iron Man*), but it's the sheer wealth of names that impresses. Joining Meryl Streep on the cabinet were Anthony Head (Brother Lassar in 2006's "School Reunion"); Harry Lloyd (Baines in 2007's "Human Nature"/"Family of Blood"); Pip Torrens (also the Headmaster in the same Tenth Doctor two-parter); Olivia Colman (mother coma victim in 2010's "The Eleventh Hour" and as herself in 2013's *The Five(ish) Doctors Reboot*); Iain Glen (Father Octavian in 2010's "The Time of Angels"/"Flesh & Stone"); Richard E. Grant (The Doctor in 1999's *The Curse of Fatal Death* and the 2003 animated adventure, *Scream of the Shalka*, Doctor Simeon in 2012's "The Snowmen"and the Great Intelligence in 2013's "The Bells of Saint John" and "The Name of the Doctor"; Rupert Vansittart (General Asquith/Slitheen in 2005's "Aliens of London"/"World War Three"); Clifford Rose (Rorvik in 1981's "Warriors' Gate"); Michael Cochrane (Charles Cranleigh in "Black Orchid" (1982) and Redvers Fenn-Cooper in 1989's "Ghost Light"); and Jim Broadbent (The Doctor in 1999's *The Curse of Fatal Death*). Phew! Now that is a cast!

A Clockwork Orange

Going back to the seventies now, and Stanley Kubrick's violent and disturbing classic snuck in a couple of *Doctor Who* notables. Detective Constable Tom, the formidable Steven Berkoff, would be familiar as the Shakri from "The Power of Three" (2012), while the less familiar Minotaur in "The Time Monster" (1972) was David Prowse, who played huge manservant Julian in the 1971 film.

Pearl Harbor

Michael Bay's wartime disaster flick (the adjective describing the quality of the film, not the content) from 2001 may have Hollywood names such as Ben Affleck, but it also featured Daniel Mays (Alex from 2011's "Night Terrors") and the previously mentioned Tony Curran (Vincent van Gogh from 2010's "Vincent and the Doctor").

The King's Speech

Back to quality now, this 2010 Academy Award–winning film saw the heavyweight actors Michael Gambon (Kazran and Elliot Sardick in 2010's "A Christmas Carol") and Derek Jacobi (Professor Yana in 2007's "Utopia") star alongside Adrian Scarborough (Kahler-Jex in 2012's "A Town Called Mercy") and, best of all, the Doctor's mother (otherwise known as The Woman) from "The End of Time" (2009–10), Claire Bloom.

Gangs of New York

Martin Scorsese's brutal retelling of the New York riots found three notable entries: Rab Affleck, who played Strax's Glaswegian fighting partner Archie in "The Name of the Doctor" (2013); Sean Gilder, the Sycorax leader in "The Christmas Invasion" (2005); and Angela Pleasence, the rather angry Queen Elizabeth at the denouement of "The Shakespeare Code" (2007).

Guardians of the Galaxy

Though Karen Gillan was quite noticeable as blue-skinned baddie Nebula (and due to return for the 2016 sequel), this 2014 Marvel romp also starred Christopher Fairbank as the Broker (he appears in Series 8, Episode 9); Spencer Wilding as the blue-skinned "Mean Guard" who likes to listen to Star Lord's headphones (Spencer played Skaldak in 2013's "Cold War" amongst other monster roles in *Who*); and Naomi Ryan as a Nova Centurion (she was Amy Pond's ill-fated makeup artist, Cassandra, in 2012's "Asylum of the Daleks").

Doctor Who Stars Who Appeared in the Batman Films

Many *Who* stars have made appearances in superhero films, but it's the Batman franchise that provides the most wealth and interesting choices. Gotham is full of friends (and enemies!) of the Doctor.

Michael Gough

The esteemed English actor played the ever-present butler Alfred Pennyworth to Bruce Wayne in the Tim Burton "dark" reimagining of Gotham's finest in *Batman* (1989). Gough would also go on to reprise the role in the Burton sequel, *Batman Returns* (1992), and the less well-received *Batman Forever* (1995) and *Batman & Robin* (1997), and has become almost as iconic as Batman himself. Similarly, in the world of *Doctor Who*, Gough was a standout character, on more than one occasion. He was the rather playful Celestial Toymaker in the William Hartnell serial "The Celestial Toymaker" (1966), and then the villainous Time Lord Hedin in "Arc of Infinity," a Peter Davison four-parter from 1983. Fact fans will also note that Gough was married to actress Anneke Wills (companion Polly) for seventeen years.

Lachele Carl

Star of television news throughout the Russell T. Davies era on *Doctor Who* (and even popping up in the spin-offs *Torchwood* and *The Sarah Jane Adventures*), Carl also worked on television news in the 1989 *Batman* film. After a news anchor breaks out into hysterical laughter (caused by the Joker) on the show *Action News*, Carl can be seen as production team member Rene requesting medical help for her fallen colleague.

Pat Gorman

In an uncredited role in the first Tim Burton Batman film, Gorman played a cop at the Axis Chemicals factory. In *Doctor Who*, he would sometimes play uncredited or unnamed roles, too. He's "starred" in numerous stories over the years from 1965 up until 1985, playing Cybermen, a UNIT soldier, as well as many other parts (alien and human!).

Garrick Hagon

Garrick, who you'll also find in a couple of other lists in this book, makes an appearance almost immediately in *Batman* (1989), playing a tourist (trying not to look like one) trying to track down a taxi with his family. The actor played Ky in "The Mutants" (a Jon Pertwee adventure from 1972) and, more recently, Abraham in the Matt Smith 2012 episode "A Town Called Mercy."

Shane Rimmer

Moving onto the newer Batman films, but staying with another actor who also appeared in *Star Wars* (and a few James Bond movies, too), Rimmer had a part as a Gotham Water Board Technician (getting a few lines) in the Christopher Nolan reboot, *Batman Begins* (2005). The Canadian actor also starred as Seth Harper in "The Gunfighters," a First Doctor tale from 1966.

Spencer Wilding

Known for his "creature" roles in the Matt Smith era (Skaldak in 2013's "Cold War," the Wooden King in 2011's "The Doctor, the Widow and the Wardrobe," and the Creature in 2011's "The God Complex"), Wilding played a warrior in the League of Shadows in *Batman Begins*.

Gerard Murphy

Staying with Christopher Nolan's first Batman outing, Murphy was the corrupt Judge Faden on the payroll of mob boss Carmine Falcone (another mob boss coming up later). In *Doctor Who*, he played Richard Maynarde, the memorable servant of Lady Peinforte, in "Silver Nemesis," a Sylvester McCoy story from the 25th Anniversary year that also featured the Cybermen.

Christine Adams

Playing the secretary to Wayne Industries' CEO in *Batman Begins*, Adams got to do some serious flirting with Bruce Wayne before she realized who he was, as he taught her how to swing. With a golf club. In the world of *Who*, the actress starred as Cathica Santini Khadeni in "The Long Game" (which aired in the same year as *Batman*, 2005). She came face to face with the Ninth Doctor and Rose, and even helped to defeat the Mighty Jagrafess of the Holy Hadrojassic Maxarodenfoe on Satellite Five during the Fourth Great and Bountiful Human Empire.

David Ajala

In an unnamed role, David Ajala played a stooge of the Joker in the 2008 sequel, *The Dark Knight*, delivering the slightly unhinged green-haired one onto fellow criminal Gambol (who was duly executed). The actor made a rather scary impression in the second Eleventh Doctor episode "The Beast Below" (2010), as Peter, the chief of the Winders.

Colin McFarlane

McFarlane played Loeb, the Commissioner of the Gotham City Police Department, in the first two Christopher Nolan Batman movies before coming to a sticky end at the hands of the Joker in *The Dark Knight*, poisoned by Scotch. He had a substantial and memorable part in *Doctor Who*, though you'll have to listen very carefully to track him down. Colin provided the voice for the Heavenly Host in the 2007 Christmas special, "Voyage of the Damned." He also starred as the morally ambiguous General Pierce in the *Doctor Who* spin-off *Torchwood: Children of Earth*.

Burn Gorman

Speaking of *Torchwood*, their very-own Owen Harper makes a brief turn in *The Dark Knight Rises*. Playing Phillip Stryver, his character also

came to a grisly end as he was sentenced to cross the icy river surrounding Gotham, which he fell through.

David Gyasi

A most definite blink-and-you'll-miss-it appearance here as Harvey from the Eleventh Doctor story "Asylum of the Daleks" (2012), Gyasi stars as "Skinny Prisoner" in *The Dark Knight Rises* (2012). He also appeared in *Torchwood* (the 2006 episode "Combat").

Eric Roberts

And to end with, let's have a biggie. Julia Roberts' brother played crime boss Sal Maroni in *The Dark Knight* and faced off against both Batman (where he was dropped from a tall building) and Harvey Dent (who had then become Two Face). Unfortunately for him, the latter meeting looks like it left him slightly dead—maybe he should have dressed for the occasion. Of course, in *Doctor Who*, he battled the Doctor himself, then played by Paul McGann, in the one-off television movie of 1996. Again, he came off second best.

Real People and the Doctor

Despite meeting many people you may never have heard of, the Doctor has met many historical and real people from our planet since his first visit so many years ago. Here, for your pleasure, are some of the more recognizable and interesting figures he's met since his travels began.

Richard Nixon

Old Tricky Dicky came to be an interesting ally for the Eleventh Doctor when he landed the TARDIS in the Oval Office in "The Impossible Astronaut" (2011) along with the Ponds and River Song back in 1969. The Silence, also a tricky lot, were causing havoc, and their young girl prisoner (Melody Pond) was making some late-night calls to the President. Given what he knew about Nixon's activities, the Time Lord was pretty chummy with the man who would go on to disgrace the United States so publicly. To his credit, Dicky did assist with Team TARDIS's battle against the memory-blasting parasites, though he wasn't so broad-minded when it came to same-sex marriages...

Barack Obama

Another American president here, and, I have to admit, this one is a bit of a cheat as the Doctor didn't actually meet Obama in person; he was transmogrified into the image of the Master during "The End of Time" (2009). Sadly, Barack's plan to help out the world's finances was never revealed—a great pity, as it's probably something we could all do with.

Winston Churchill

Ah, Winnie was a good old friend of the Doctor and felt at ease to call him up whenever he needed some assistance, as seen at the end of "The Beast Below" (2010). During World War II, his "Ironsides" were the Daleks who turned against the Prime Minister, but, with the Eleventh Doctor and Amy's help, the rebellion was quashed. Winston's brave attitude in the face of adversity was summed up by his own words, "K.B.O.—Keep Buggering On." Churchill helped his

friend out again when Van Gogh's painting came into his hands, calling on River Song to contact the Time Lord.

Vincent Van Gogh

Poor Vincent, such a sensitive soul. The Eleventh Doctor took Amy Pond to meet the painter after a visit to a gallery revealed a rather unpleasant looking alien, the Krafayis, in one of his paintings during "Vincent and the Doctor" (2010). Vincent's mental illness was apparent, and though the time-traveling couple tried to buoy his spirits, the artist's life still came to a sad end, though not before he had the chance to send a chilling warning to the Doctor in his painting *The Pandorica Opens*.

Leonardo da Vinci

Hundreds of years previous to his meeting with Van Gogh, the Doctor was familiar with another painter, Leonardo da Vinci (who was also not bad at the odd invention, too). The Fourth Doctor nearly bumped into him during "The Masque of Mandragora" (1976), and it was only a few years later when the same incarnation of the Time Lord traveled to meet Leonardo and left him a very familiar note, referring to him as "Leo" in "City of Death" (1979). At some point in their friendship, Da Vinci gave the Doctor a calling card, as seen in "The Two Doctors" (1985). Matt Smith's Eleventh Doctor would cite the inventor's dyslexia to Elliot in "The Hungry Earth" (2010) in the hope of encouraging him.

Leo also popped up in the diary of the Monk (a renegade Time Lord) in the William Hartnell story "The Time Meddler" (1965), and his sketches can be seen in the Patrick Troughton tale "The Seeds of Death" (1969) and in the 1996 Paul McGann TV Movie (in Grace Holloway's home).

Charles Dickens

The famous writer and the Gallifreyan, as with many of his relationships, got off to a rocky start. The Ninth Doctor and Rose Tyler had taken a trip to Cardiff in 1869 (though the intention was actually to visit Naples in 1860) and found Dickens at the center of an attack by the Gelth during "The Unquiet Dead" (2005). Charlie, as the Time Lord referred to him, was slightly put off with the way he was addressed by his "fan"—and the Doctor was a big fan (of most of his work, at any rate). By the end of their time together, their friendship was assured, though, sadly, there was not much life left in the writer.

William Shakespeare

Another writer and, arguably, one slightly more famous than the above entry. Before the two men came face to face, the First Doctor showed off his Time and Space Visualizer in "The Chase" (1965) to Vicki, Ian, and Barbara, using a conversation between Shakespeare, Queen Elizabeth I, and Francis Bacon as evidence of his wondrous machine's capabilities. The tenth incarnation of the Gallifreyan took Martha Jones to meet the man in "The Shakespeare Code" (2007), who took quite a shine to his "Dark Lady," citing "Shall I compare thee to a summer's day?" Willy saved the day with his words (and a smidgen of help from J.K. Rowling) against the Carrionites but was unfazed by the alienness of his newfound traveler. The Doctor also gifted the Bard with a new word, "Sycorax," which he would go on to use in *The Tempest* (a play the Time Lord misquoted on the planet Deva Loka).

Agatha Christie

Writer number three! A trip to the twentieth century with Donna Noble saw the Tenth Doctor face a frosty Agatha in "The Unicorn and the Wasp" (2008). Her own fictitious crime stories became the basis of how the alien, a giant wasp, attacked and killed its prey. Like with Dickens and Shakespeare, the Doctor was also a huge fan of Christie's work, and in the end seemed to be the cause of her infamous "missing" ten days.

Wyatt Earp

Well known worldwide as the Marshal who took part in the infamous Gunfight at the O.K. Corral in Tombstone, Arizona, the First Doctor confessed that he "always wanted to meet" Earp when they met in "The Gunfighters" (1966). The Time Lord had been suffering a nasty bout of toothache when he crossed paths with the gun-toting lawman, who sent him on to his friend Doc Holliday, another real-life historical person. Fact fans may note that Wyatt Earp's middle names were "Berry Stapp."

Alexander Graham Bell

Though not actually seen in an episode, his voice can be heard in "Father's Day" (2005) as time goes wonky. Listen closely to Rose's mobile phone and you can hear Bell's first phone call to his assistant.

It's Not Stealing, It's an Homage!

Doctor Who hasn't been shy about borrowing from other genres, and has done so many times since 1963—some more obvious than others. Here's when *Who* paid tribute to its sources.

Episode	Inspiration
"Planet of Giants"(1964)	*Gulliver's Travels*
"Inferno" (1970)	*Quatermass*
"Robot" (1974–75)	*King Kong*
"Planet of Evil" (1975)	*Forbidden Planet/Dr. Jekyll and Mr. Hyde*
"The Android Invasion" (1975)	*Invasion of the Body Snatchers*
"The Brain of Morbius" (1976)	*Frankenstein*
"The Seeds of Doom" (1976)	*The Thing/The Day of the Triffids*
"The Deadly Assassin" (1976)	*The Manchurian Candidate*
"The Invisible Enemy" (1977)	*Fantastic Voyage*
"The Robots of Death" (1964)	*Ten Little Indians/The Mousetrap*
"The Talons of Weng-Chiang" (1977)	*Sherlock Holmes/Fu-Manchu*
"The Androids of Tara" (1978)	*The Prisoner of Zenda*
"The Caves of Androzani" (1984)	*The Phantom of the Opera*
"Terror of the Vervoids" (1986)	*Murder on the Orient Express*
"Paradise Towers" (1987)	*High-Rise by JG Ballard*
"Voyage of the Damned" (2007)	*The Poseidon Adventure*
"The Unicorn and the Wasp" (2008)	Agatha Christie
"A Christmas Carol" (2010)	*A Christmas Carol*
"The Doctor, the Widow and the Wardrobe" (2011)	*The Lion, the Witch and the Wardrobe*
"Into the Dalek" (2014)	*Fantastic Voyage*

The Doctor, the Widow and the Wardrobe

Honorable Mention

Since 2005, *Doctor Who* has adapted other works for the screen, most notably:

- **"Dalek"** (2005): based on Robert Shearman's Big Finish Productions audio adventure *Jubilee*

- **"Rise of the Cybermen"/"Age of Steel"** (2006): inspired by Marc Platt's audio adventure *Spare Parts*

- **"Human Nature"/"Family of Blood"** (2007): based on Paul Cornell's Virgin New Adventures novel, *Human Nature*

TV Shows That *Doctor Who* References

Just as many television shows like to name-check or mention the TARDIS or Daleks, *Doctor Who* is not shy of paying props to other shows from our little planet. Again, not every show referenced is cited here.

The Hitchhiker's Guide to the Galaxy

Unsurprisingly, given that author Douglas Adams worked on *Who* as a writer and script editor, some references to his hilarious and well-loved creation wormed their way onto the show. As soon as he became script editor, Adams used "Destiny of the Daleks" (1979) to name-check Betelgeuse and Oolon Coluphid (and its book *Origins of the Universe*). More recently, a species from the *Hitchhiker's Guide*, the Hooloovoo, turned up at the Festival of Offerings in "The Rings of Akhaten" (2013). Another "in universe," and more obvious one, came in David Tennant's first special, "The Christmas Invasion" (2005), when the Tenth Doctor commented, "Very Arthur Dent. Now, there was a nice man." The Time Lord, as you will remember, was dressed only in pajamas and a dressing gown for the majority of the adventure against the Sycorax— much like the "hero" of *The Hitchhiker's Guide to the Galaxy*.

There are more oblique references to the series: with the Seventh Doctor asking in "Ghost Light" (1993): "Who was it said Earthmen never invite their ancestors round to dinner?" (A nod to "Earthmen are not proud of their ancestors, and never invite them round to dinner," from *The Guide*); the number 42 (the answer to the question of life, the universe, and everything in the Adams books) popping up in another Tenth Doctor Christmas special, 2007's "Voyage of the Damned," not to mention an episode titled after the number, though this was for a different reason); in 2011's "The Doctor's Wife" (penned by Neil Gaiman, a Douglas Adams fan who wrote the book *Don't Panic: The Official Hitchhikers Guide to the Galaxy Companion*), the phrases "plughole at the end of the universe" and "scrap yard at the end of the universe" are used—a knowing wink to the second of the Hitchhiker's series, *The Restaurant at the End of the Universe*; and, finally, in the Library (from 2008's "Silence in the Library"/"Forest of the Dead") there is a copy of *The Hitchhiker's Guide to the Galaxy*, just what Douglas would have wanted.

Fact fans will note that the Fifth Doctor, Peter Davison, starred as the Dish of the Day in the final episode of the series.

The X Factor

Nasty Lance Bennett revealed, in a rather long list, that the British "singing" competition was a favorite of his nearly wife Donna Noble in "The Runaway Bride" (2006). This was something that irked him. Poor lad. He's dead now, so it's ok.

Scooby-Doo

From the veritable sublime to the utterly ridiculous. Who would have thought the dog detective would have such a profound influence in the world of *Doctor Who*? In the 2006 Cybermen two-parter, Peter Tyler refers to Ricky's gang, the Preachers, as "Scooby-Doo and his gang. They've even got the van." In the Steven Moffat story "Blink," Larry Nightingale used the phrase "Scooby-Doo's house" to describe the building in which Sally Sparrow discovered the Weeping Angels. Best of all, however, was the mention in another Moffat tale, 1999's Comic Relief special, "The Curse of Fatal Death." Comparing one to the other, the Doctor's assistant Emma says (when she thinks the Time Lord is dying), "You're like Father Christmas, the Wizard of Oz, Scooby-Doo. And I love you very much. And we all need you, and you simply cannot die." Though not mentioned in the story itself, some of the UK press compared (rather unfavorably) the Vashta Nerada (from "Silence in the Library") inhabiting the space suit to a Scooby-Doo villain.

The Apprentice

English entrepreneur Lord Sugar (formerly Sir Alan Sugar), host of the UK money-grabbing reality show, made an appearance in 2012's "The Power of Three," encouraging contestants to find a use for the mysterious black boxes that had suddenly appeared on the planet. The Doctor was clearly a fan of the man and just the year before, in "The God Complex," he turned to Amy and used big Al's catchphrase, "with regret, you're fired," when finding a potential new companion, Rita.

Star Trek

The long-running franchise (but not as long as *Doctor Who*) has made its mark on the Whoniverse. In the Ninth Doctor episode "The Empty Child," Rose Tyler complained about the Time Lord's lack of "tech," pleading with him, "Give me some Spock, for once!" (In case you don't know, Spock is an officer on the USS *Enterprise*.) Her wish came true when Captain Jack Harkness came along with fancy gadgets that were "very Spock," and she even introduced the Gallifreyan as Mister Spock to the handsome Time Agent. Spock is the focus of another reference in the next series with the Tenth Doctor. Upon meeting Chloe Webber, he tried to teach her the Vulcan salute in "Fear Her."

During the Eleventh Doctor's time, there were more allusions to the sci-fi series. In 2011's "The Impossible Astronaut," Joy bumped into a Silent in the White House toilets and asked, "Is that a mask? Is that a *Star Trek* thing?" shortly before being vaporized. Later that year, Howie Spragg in "The God Complex" found some attractive girls in Room 155 and was asked what "loser" is in Klingon, while just an episode later, in "Closing Time," Craig Owens used the well-worn "Beam me up!" from the original *Star Trek* series.

Amusingly, in "The Pandorica Opens" (2010), a rather rusty Cyberman threatened Amy Pond with "You will be assimilated!"—a catchphrase also used by *Star Trek: The Next Generation* goons, the Borg. And, as we all know, the Borg are nothing but poor knock-offs of The Cybermen.

The Clangers/The Teletubbies

For those unaware, both of these are British children's shows: the former from the sixties and seventies and the latter from the nineties. And both share one common factor: the Master is a huge fan. In the Third Doctor adventure "The Sea Devil," 1972, the evil bearded one (played by Roger Delgado) can be seen enjoying an episode of *The Clangers*, while his future self (John Simm) takes in *The Teletubbies* in the Series 3 finale before unleashing The Toclafane on planet Earth.

Eastenders

And for those outside the UK, *Eastenders* is a "soap" based in London, which began on the BBC in 1985. Some twenty-one years later, *Doctor Who* packed in two big old mentions for the show. In "The Impossible Planet," after Ida Scott has proclaimed, "There's no turning back," (having traveled down to the core of Krop Tor), the Tenth Doctor says, "No turning back? That's almost as bad as nothing can possibly go wrong, or this is going to be the best Christmas Walford's ever had." (Walford is the fictional area of London where Eastenders is set.) A few episodes later in "Army of Ghosts," we find that the titular ghosts (actually Cybermen) have not only made an impression on the world but also on the soap, with the ghost of former character Den Watts (played by Leslie Grantham, who helped Davros out in 1984's "Resurrection of the Daleks") returning to "haunt" his old pub.

And when it came to the Eleventh Doctor's tenure, Amy and Rory were no slouches on giving the nod. "The Doctor's back there in Eastenders-land" came Rory's response to the block of flats they found themselves in during "Night Terrors" (2011).

It would be remiss of me not to mention the mind-bending 3-D cross-over for Children in Need during Doctor Who's 30th Anniversary, "Dimensions In Time," that saw the various incarnations of the Doctor get together with his companions to fight the Rani while humping around Albert Square and its sorry denizens. But the less people see the Doctors and his companions, the better. Truly awful.

Blue Peter

Another children's show from the BBC, and none can boast such a strong and lengthy connection with *Doctor Who*. In the eighties, Seventh Doctor companion Ace brandishes two Blue Peter badges during her travels (actress Sophie Aldred, who played Ace, actually won them in her younger years), while in 2005, during "Aliens of London," a television in the Tyler household can be seen to be showing *Blue Peter*, where presenter Matt Baker demonstrates how to make a tasty alien spaceship cake.

Of course, the bond between the two beloved shows goes further, even providing monsters for *Who* (the Abzorbaloff in 2006's "Love & Monsters"), set design (the junkyard TARDIS in 2011's "The Doctor's Wife"), and weapons (sonic devices for Team Vastra in the first series with Peter Capaldi as the Time Lord) —all designed by *Blue Peter* viewers in competitions.

Almost every actor who has played the Doctor has appeared on the show, sometimes judging competitions, and even presenter Peter Purves starred as William Hartnell's companion, Steven Taylor, in the sixties. Unlike *Doctor Who*, however, where several seasons, stories, and episodes have been lost through time (and videotape/film reuse), every episode of *Blue Peter* exists in the BBC archives.

The Addams Family

To help the Doctor from an impending crash with a train, Clara simply says, "Addams Family," as a solution. Seconds later, the Time Lord's hand is seen coming out of the TARDIS (now shrunk), crawling and dragging the time machine with it. The Gallifreyan was obviously a fan of Thing, the iconic hand from the 1960s show.

That Does Not Compute!

52

Computers have been a feature of *Doctor Who* almost since its inception, so it's no surprise to see a long and strong association with computer games. Included here are all of the "officially licensed" computer games (some available only in the UK) released to celebrate the show.

Doctor Who: The First Adventure (1983)

Peter Davison's Fifth Doctor adorned the cover of this debut for the Time Lord in the gaming world that featured *Doctor Who* versions of already popular video games, such as Pac-Man and Space Invaders. Available only for the BBC Micro, the game also featured "invisible monsters" lurking in the Box of Tantalus.

Doctor Who and the Warlord (1985)

The next release from BBC Software claimed on the back cover, "Using your intelligence, fluency and good looks you will need to think, talk and charm your way out of scores of mind-wrenching situations and collect the objects essential to completing the game." It was a "text adventure" game that relied on typing in instructions (the eighties were a crazy time).

Doctor Who and the Mines of Terror (1986)

This more colorful and complex game for the BBC Micro, Amstrad, and Commodore 64 featured the Sixth Doctor and companion Splinx.

Dalek Attack (1992)

Doctor Who had been off the air for a couple of years, but *Dalek Attack* kept the legend alive. Available for a number of computer systems (all obsolete now), this was a platform shoot-'em-up where you could choose to be either the Second, Fourth, or Seventh Doctor. The blurb boasted: "The Daleks have conquered most of the Universe, their reign of terror must be stopped..."

Destiny of the Doctors (1997)

Available on PC CD-Rom, this was a 3-D adventure starring Anthony Ainley in specially recorded scenes as the Master. *Destiny of the Doctors* also featured Daleks, Ice Warriors, Cybermen, and more as you sought to free the Doctor's seven selves from the clutches of the bearded renegade Time Lord. *Doctor Who* VHS releases at the time even included trailers for the game!

Top Trumps: Doctor Who (2008)

For the Nintendo Wii, this baffling entry into *Who* games is, well, baffling. Top Trumps is already a game—a card game! Why on earth anyone thought this was a good idea is beyond comprehension.

The Adventure Games (2010–11)

Free games! (Well, in the UK anyway—sorry, U.S.!) And damn good they are, too. Online games *City of the Daleks, Blood of the Cybermen, TARDIS, Shadows of the Vashta Nerada,* and *The Gunpowder Plot* star Matt Smith and Karen Gillan and were written by such talented authors as Phil Ford (2009's "The Waters of Mars") and James Moran (2008's "The Fires of Pompeii"). They are still available on the official *Doctor Who* website.

Evacuation Earth and Return to Earth (2010)

Released simultaneously for the Nintendo DS and Wii respectively, these two entries did not set the gaming world alight. The former was playable but the latter won the honor of "Worst Wii Game of 2010," and was awarded a 19-percent rating from the *Official Nintendo Magazine.*

Mazes of Time (2010)

Unlike the games of its time, this Eleventh Doctor release for iOS and Android doesn't feature the voice cast of *Doctor Who,* though it does feature Daleks, Cybermen, and Silurians among other foes.

Cleric Wars (2012)

Another title for iOS and Android, *Cleric Wars* is a free augmented reality game that requires a special gun attachment for your phone to work properly. You get to zap Weeping Angels!

The Eternity Clock (2012)

Featuring Matt Smith and Alex Kingston, this game was released for PS3, PS Vita, and PC, and includes a TARDIS full of *Doctor Who* continuity for fans. Sadly, *The Eternity Clock* saw the end to further installments of *The Adventure Games* on the official site.

Worlds in Time (2012)

Featuring Autons, Zygons, Daleks, Cybermen, Clockwork Droids, and Weeping Angels, this was a fun game for the younger player and was the first-ever multiplayer online *Doctor Who* game.

Legacy (2013)

This most recent release came hot on the heels of the 50th Anniversary and is available on iOS and Android. With over one million downloads, this puzzle game is constantly being updated and involves the online community in future choices. *Legacy* was voted by the *Guardian* newspaper as one of the top fifty Android and iPhone/iPad apps in 2013.

The Doctor Is Coming

53

The popular, and slightly less family-oriented, HBO show *Game of Thrones* shares a huge amount of talent with *Doctor Who*, and you can catch them all below!

Actor	*Game of Thrones*	*Doctor Who*
Julian Glover	Grand Maester Pycelle	Richard the Lionheart, "The Crusade" (1965) and Scaroth, "City of Death" (1979)
Iain Glen	Ser Jorah Mormont	Father Octavian, "The Time of Angels"/"Flesh and Stone" (2010)
Spencer Wilding	White Walker	Various creatures, "The Doctor, the Widow and the Wardrobe" (2011), "The God Complex" (2011), and "Cold War" (2013)
Liam Cunningham	Ser Davos Seaworth	Captain Zhukov, "Cold War" (2013)

Actor	Game of Thrones	Doctor Who
Diana Rigg	Olenna Tyrell	Winifred Gillyflower, "The Crimson Horror" (2013)
Harry Lloyd	Viserys Targaryen	Baines, "Human Nature"/"The Family of Blood" (2007)
Thomas Sangster	Jojen Reed	Tim Latimer "Human Nature"/"The Family of Blood" (2007)
Joe Dempsie	Gendry	Cline, "The Doctor's Daughter" (2008)
Robert Pugh	Craster	Tony Mack, "The Hungry Earth"/ "Cold Blood" (2010)
Donald Sumpter	Maester Luwin	Enrico Casali, "The Wheel in Space" (1968) and Ridgeway, "The Sea Devils" (1972)
Ian Hanmore	Pyat Pree	Father Angelo, "Tooth and Claw" (2006)
Tobias Menzies	Edmure Tully	Lieutenant Stepashin, "Cold War" (2013)
Mark Gatiss	Tycho Nestoris	Professor Richard Lazarus, "The Lazarus Experiment" (2007)
David Bradley	Walder Frey	Solomon, "Dinosaurs on a Spaceship" (2012)

Actor	Game of Thrones	Doctor Who
Ron Donachie	Rodrik Cassel	Steward, "Tooth and Claw" (2006)
Lucian Msamati	Salladhor Saan	Guido, "The Vampires of Venice" (2010)
Mark Killeen	Mero	German Officer, "Let's Kill Hitler" (2011)
Tim Plester	Black Walder Frey	Solomon, "Dinosaurs on a Spaceship" (2012)
David Verrey	High Septon	Joseph Green, "Aliens of London"/"World War Three" (2005)
Margaret John	Old Nan	Grandma Connolly, "The Idiot's Lantern" (2006)
Sam Callis	Gold Cloak	Security Guard, "Bad Wolf" (2005)
Paul Bentley	High Septon	Professor Candy, "Let's Kill Hitler" (2011)
Sean Buckley	Old Man	Barman, "The Wedding of River Song" (2011)
Jamie Sives	Jory Cassel	Captain Reynolds, "Tooth and Claw" (2006)
Owen Teale	Ser Alliser Thorne	Maldak, "Vengeance on Varos" (1985)
David Fynn	Rennick	Marcellus, "The Pandorica Opens" (2010)
Roger Ashton-Griffiths	Mace Tyrell	Quayle, "Robot of Sherwood" (2014)

Fact fans will note that the unaired Game of Thrones pilot featured Ian McNeice, who played the Eleventh Doctor's chum Winston Churchill.

54

TV Shows That Reference *Doctor Who*

During its initial run from the sixties to the eighties, many British shows referenced or name-checked *Doctor Who*. But, as you will see here, many television series from North America started to pay homage to the Doctor from the nineties onward. We don't have the time and space to feature every reference, but here are some of the more unusual and fun.

Seinfeld

During *Doctor Who*'s 30th Anniversary, one of the greatest U.S. sitcoms snuck in a treat for the more eagle-eyed viewers. In the 1993 episode "The Smelly Car," a copy of "Revenge of the Cybermen" (1975) on VHS can be seen on the shelf in Champagne Video, the video rental store of choice for Jerry and his friends. Four years later, and in the same shop, the William Hartnell classic "The Web Planet" (1965) is a new addition in "The Comeback." Reportedly responsible for these choices was staff writer Darin Henry, who would go on to write the *Doctor Who* audio drama *The Game* (starring Peter Davison). Seinfeld also boasts a couple of *Who* stars in the shape of Guy Siner (Kaled military officer Ravon in 1975's "Genesis of the Daleks") and Mike McShane (Weeping Angel collector Julius Grayle in 2012's "The Angels Take Manhattan").

The Sarah Silverman Show

Now this is quite a remarkable reference. The short-lived U.S. sitcom featured an appearance from none other than the Ninth Doctor himself, Christopher Eccleston, who starred as Dr. Lazer Rage from a fictional sci-fi show called *Dr. Lazer Rage*, appearing on the cover of a DVD box set of the show. Considering his reluctance to return to or discuss *Doctor Who*, this is a gem of a cameo from Eccleston.

Leverage

A strange choice but the crime-fighting series clearly had *Who* fans in their ranks. Throughout Leverage's four-year run, some familiar aliases were used by the main characters, including Tom Baker and Sarah Jane; Rose; Moffat and Davies (as in Steven and Russell T., two of *Doctor Who*'s show runners); Agents Smith and Tennant (Matt and David, the Tenth and Eleventh Doctors); and Sally Sparrow (from 2007's "Blink").

But there's more. The *Leverage* team came across a law firm called McGann, McCoy, and Baker (the surnames of the Eighth, Seventh, Sixth, and Fourth Doctors), while the character Hardison, clearly a fan, even said "bow ties are cool" in an episode (and also complained about the time taken to download the latest episode). Actress Gina Bellman stars as Sophie Devereaux in Leverage but was once the muse of Steven Moffat, having starred in every episode of his sitcom, *Coupling*. And, for completion, actor Mark A. Sheppard (who plays Sterling), is Canton Everett Delaware III in the Eleventh Doctor two-parter, "The Impossible Astronaut"/"Day of the Moon" (2011).

Futurama

Matt Groening's "other" show, the sci-fi-anim-sitcom, showed a fondness for *Who* on a couple of outings for the Planet Express crew. Most obviously, in the 2011 episode "All The Presidents' Heads," we see the TARDIS and the Fourth Doctor (there's also a flying red bus in there, too, which could be a sly wink to 2009's "Planet of the Dead"), while the same episode also sees the names Amelia Pond and Owen Harper (from the *Torchwood* team) used for *Futurama*'s notorious heads-in-jars. Later that same year, Tom Baker's incarnation of the Time Lord crops up again, emerging from the mouth of a huge space whale in an homage to the denouement of Steven Spielberg's film *Close Encounters of the Third Kind*. And, of course, one of the crew of Planet Express is called Leela!

The Big Bang Theory

Over the years, this hugely popular sitcom has screened many, many episodes with *Doctor Who* nods so we'll keep it brief. Sheldon reveals that every Saturday he wakes up at 6:15 am to watch *Doctor Who*, while occasionally, a Dalek can be seen on his shelf in his apartment. In said apartment, the gang can be seen watching "Silence in the Library" (2008), when Amy (Sheldon's "girlfriend") remarks on the Time Lord's fondness for contemporary London (which was odd, given the episode they were actually watching). Posters have popped up in places like the comic book store (no real surprise there, as the owner, Stuart, once dressed up as the Fourth Doctor) and also in Raj's apartment. Rajesh Koothrappali also shows his love for *Who* when he gets a TARDIS to complement his Halloween party. There's more but our definite favorite is when Howard Wolowitz sings a song to his wife that includes the lyrics, "I'd be *Doctor Who* without the TARDIS." Awwww.

Criminal Minds

Another surprise here as we find the American show with a FBI team of profilers indulging in some *Who* fun. The show managed two episodes in 2011 with references: in "Dorado Falls," the team is on the lookout for someone who attended a *Doctor Who* convention in San Diego, while Spencer Reid puts to rights the *Bill & Ted*/*Doctor Who* argument in "Coda." Best of all is the Season 7 finale in 2012 where the aforementioned Reid is dressed as the Fourth Doctor while his associate is dressed as a female version of the Eleventh Doctor at a sci-fi convention where they meet a couple of other *Who* cosplayers (policewoman Amy and the Eleventh Doctor).

Community

A special hats off to the college-based sitcom. These guys and girls went one beyond tribute and mere references by creating their own fictional show, *Inspector Spacetime*. Their sci-fi series, which begins in 1962, features a classic British red phone box and sees an eccentrically dressed Englishman (the Inspector) traveling through space and time in said phone box with an assistant. *Community* repeatedly shows clips from the "show," while posters of *Inspector Spacetime* adorn the walls of Abed and Troy's apartment. The former of the two actually makes specific references to *Doctor Who*, however, comparing himself to K9 and also wearing a TARDIS shirt in one episode. In the "real" world, actress Karen Gillan stated she wanted to star in episode of *Community* or *Inspector Spacetime*.

My Little Pony: Friendship is Magic

Even *My Little Pony* honors the world's greatest television show. Occasionally, a male Earth pony called Time Turner, also known as Doctor Whooves, makes an appearance. In 2014, he was seen wearing 3-D glasses (à la the Tenth Doctor in 2006's "Army of Ghosts"/"Doomsday") while accompanied by a female pony, a rose "cutie mark"—an obvious nod to Rose Tyler.

The Simpsons

Matt Groening again. The man is obviously a fan. There's been quite the collection of references to *Doctor Who* over the years. We won't list them all, but here are some of the best (and some you may have missed). As with *Futurama*, the Fourth Doctor has cameo'd a number of times, the first in 1995 in Sideshow Bob's "Last Gleaming" (as an "esteemed representatives of television") and another notable turn in "Treehouse of Horror X," where the Time Lord had been captured and sealed in plastic by the Collector (aka Comic Book Guy). Comic Book Guy would also claim that a wheelbarrow full of tacos would "provide adequate sustenance for the *Doctor Who* marathon."

One of the more subtle tips of the hat comes in the opening credits of "Treehouse of Horror XX," which includes the name Don "He Will Knock 4 Times" Payne (airing in the same year as 2009's "Planet of the

Dead," where the prophecy was made). Likewise, another that may have sneaked passed you more recently was the 2014 episode "Diggs," which featured a plaster cast with "THE TARDIS" and "DALEK #7" inscribed on it (as a further reference, the character with the plaster cast was in an asylum—2012's "Asylum of the Daleks" aired during Series 7 of *Doctor Who*).

More obvious homages came in the 2011 *Simpsons* Christmas special, where two Daleks appeared in front of the St. Beatles Cathedral and the Benny Hilton, and in "Love Is a Many Splintered Thing" (2013), the TARDIS can be seen in a *Love Actually* spoof (and if you listen carefully, you can also hear *Sherlock*'s Benedict Cumberbatch in the episode).

Of course, the admiration is reciprocal. In Tenth Doctor story "Planet of the Ood" (2008), the "comedy classic option" setting on an Ood translator reveals the Homer Simpson annoyed grunt, "D'oh!" while in "The End of Time," the Tenth Doctor uses the phrase "Worst. Rescue. Ever!" a neat nod to Comic Book Guy's own catchphrase.

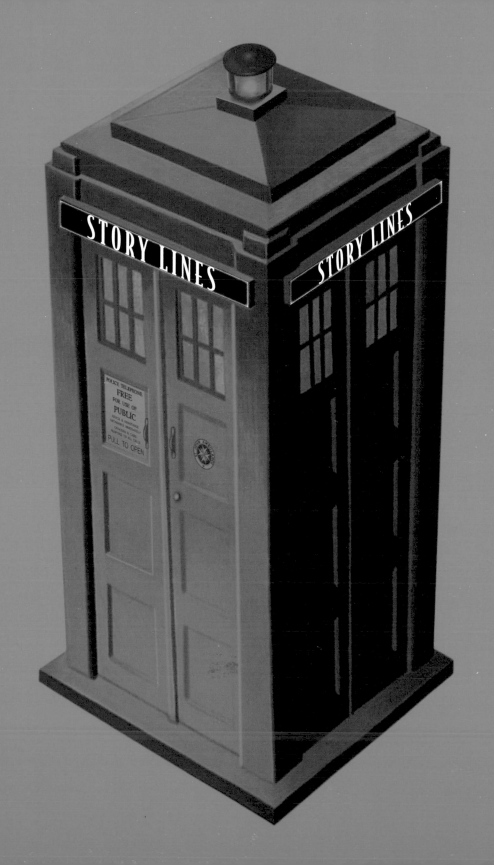

9 Underappreciated New *Doctor Who* Stories

You can check out the undervalued "classic" *Doctor Who* stories on page 151. Here, it's the turn of the new series!

"Planet of the Dead" (2009)

Considering how bold and "out there" this one-hour episode is, the amount of derision this David Tennant Easter special receives kind of baffles me. Gareth Roberts and Russell T. Davies produced a romptacular spectacular with planet-hopping on a bus! The Tritovore made for an interesting and friendly alien, but it was the unnamed, nasty, flying stingray-like creatures, devouring planets and creating their own wormholes, who chomped through the romp most threateningly.

"Aliens of London"/"World War Three" (2005)

Okay, so some of you don't like the Slitheen. I'm not a fan of *Game of Thrones*, but I don't go on about it. For the first time in *Who*'s history, we got a proper alien-invasion story that involved the world, and we saw this evidenced (through what would become a Russell T. Davies trademark, rolling news items), witnessing the ramifications on the population, not just the Doctor and his companion. The crashing of the ship into Big Ben and then into the Thames was a marvelous slice of imagery and an iconic moment for the show, displaying its newfound ability to utilize special effects convincingly. And who doesn't love the Space Pig?

"Dreamland" (2009)

You might think I'm cheating with this one, but this is a bona fide *Doctor Who* story from the BBC and even broadcast on television. From "The Waters of Mars" co-writer Phil Ford, a companion-less Tenth Doctor goes on a computer-generated animated adventure into the heart of Area 51 in the late 1950s, where the Time Lord discovers some Men in Black and a nasty alien at work. Cast-wise, this tale is quite the eye (or ear, rather) opener. There's Georgia Moffett (2008's "The Doctor's Daughter"), screen legend David Warner (*Tron*), Stuart Milligan (President Nixon in 2011's "The Impossible Astronaut" two-parter), Lisa Bowerman (familiar to some as Bernice Summerfield in the Big Finish audio adventures), and even Nicholas Rowe ("well known" for portraying Sherlock Holmes in Steven Spielberg's *Young*

April 17th, 1941

PICTURE
POST

Sherlock Holmes). Fact fans may also note that *The Sarah Jane Adventures* used elements of "Dreamland" in the Phil Ford stories "Prisoner of the Judoon" and "The Vault of Secrets."

"The Unicorn and the Wasp" (2008)

Due to its humor and light tone, a trait loathed by certain parts of *Doctor Who* fandom, this Gareth Roberts story breezes along, and is a triumph, by and large, down to the cast and the fun script. The story itself, a knowing Agatha Christie pastiche (perhaps a little too much, at times), has got laughs and giggles galore, and the cast features legends like Felicity Kendall and Christopher Benjamin and top-acting talent Tom Goodman-Hill and the beautiful Fenella Woolgar (as the aforementioned real-life crime writer). But it's that delightful chemistry of Tennant and Tate who make for the most entertaining of comedy duos, kissing and deducing their way through this summer picnic of a *Who* story.

"Boom Town" (2005)

The Slitheen! Again! Though, it should be noted, the beasts from Raxacoricofallapatorius barely make an appearance in their true form, leaving wonderful actress Annette Badland to strut her stuff so brilliantly across this episode. Never before, or since, in *Doctor Who* have we seen the Doctor—here played by everyone's favorite grumpy Northerner, Christopher Eccleston—dine with his prey before execution. "Dinner and bondage. Works for me," leers the alien during a fascinating tête-à-tête where the morality of the Doctor is laid bare by his captor in a Cardiff restaurant—the sublime meets the ridiculous (you can choose which is which in that metaphor).

"Victory of the Daleks" (2010)

I had to be in the minority when the new Dalek Paradigm came along. I was quite fond of their colorful and rotund appearance (being a fan of the Peter Cushing movie Daleks, you see) but this Mark Gatiss tale featuring the Eleventh Doctor has lots more going on than simply giant, gaudy pepperpots. Churchill, spitfires in space, and tea-serving subservient Daleks—it's got it all! In all seriousness, the notion of the mad little tanks scheming around, luring the Doctor in to reboot their species (or something like that) reminds us how clever the Daleks can be.

"Love & Monsters" (2006)

Until the appearance of Peter Kay as the Abzorbaloff in the final third of this 2006 episode starring Marc Warren, "Love and Monsters" could have been an out-and-out classic loved by all. The very notion of a "Doctor-lite" story is, without wanting to lay on this overused word, genius. Wanting to focus on the "other" people affected by the

Doctor's life is admirable and, indeed, here it's utterly fantastic—typical Russell T. Davies and typically emotional and engaging as a result. And what a cast, too! Shirley Henderson, Simon Greenall, Moya Brady, and Kathryn Drysdale add beautifully to LINDA (London Investigation 'n' Detective Agency), while Camille Coduri give us so much more with Jackie Tyler, and how it feels when left daughterless. Praise should be delivered for sheer balls and ingenuity, reinvigorating *Doctor Who* in such a thoughtful and pleasing fashion. *And* there's ELO—perfect!

"The End of the World" (2005)

It's easy to forget about this little beauty, as its previous story, "Rose," tends to get much more attention (for good reason). After showing us modern-day London, Russell T. Davies took us far into the future to watch Earth burn, but also to watch how the Ninth Doctor and his new companion were getting on. Like a couple of entries here, it was an Agatha Christie-style tale, and again in space—a simple, solid story. Rose was still coming to terms with her new BFF and their relationship was a little frosty, but after the revelation of the Time War and the need for some chips, all was well. Only two stories in and the new cast and crew were assuredly steering the show in the right direction with story and heart.

"The End of Time" (2009–10)

Lots of negativity was hurtled toward David Tennant's swan song as the Doctor, mainly due to its protracted denouement, but as a finale, "The End of Time" is nothing short of breathtaking. The good-bye scenes, which many loathed (and by many, I mean a few people on the Internet—not real people), are a testament to the Russell T. Davies era and how far we'd come in *Doctor Who*. The Time Lord cares about humans, and cares about those he travels with and those whose lives he has touched—these final moments are beautiful and incredibly moving. We are unapologetic about that, as they are stunning scenes in *Who*'s history. But "The End of Time" is so much more than the farewells; there's the bold and much-longed-for return of the Master *and* the Time Lords. The renegade's insanity is revealed, as is the macabre nature of the Doctor's people, graphically detailed in the final days of the Time War. For some, the show would never be the same again.

For Whom the Bell Tolls!

For many, the sound of the Cloister Bell is one of *the* sounds of *Doctor Who*, and it's interesting to see how little it was used back in the classic years—just three times between 1963 and 1989. Compare that to now, when we get it almost every year!

"Logopolis" (1981)

"Castrovalva" (1982)

"Resurrection of the Daleks" (1984)

"Doctor Who" (1996)

"The Sound of Drums" (2007)

"Turn Left" (2008)

"The Waters of Mars" (2009)

"The Eleventh Hour" (2010)

"The Curse of the Black Spot" (2011)

"The Doctor's Wife" (2011)

"The God Complex" (2011)

"Hide" (2013)

"Journey to the Centre of the TARDIS" (2013)

"The Name of the Doctor" (2013)

Honorable Mention

- **Children in Need special** (2005)
- **"Time Crash"** (2007)

10 Kisses from the Doctor

His earlier regenerations weren't so keen on smooching, but when he traveled to San Francisco, the Time Lord partied like it was 1999, got all smoochy, and didn't stop! Please find for your perusal some of the Time Lord's conquests over the years—though most actually conquered him.

Amy Pond

Blimey, she was a feisty one! No sooner had Amy just survived an attack by the Weeping Angels than she was rather forcibly trying to seduce the Eleventh Doctor in her bedroom in "Flesh And Stone" (2010). Despite her approaching marriage to the beaky one, Rory, Amy seemed to forget her impending nuptials as the young Scot tried it on with the Gallifreyan. "A" for effort.

Jenny Flint

After saving his life from the "crimson horror" in, well, "The Crimson Horror" (2013), Vastra's pal Jenny got a long and hard kiss from the Eleventh Doctor as thanks. But Miss Flint (or Mrs. Vastra) wasn't so keen and retaliated with her own physicality—a huge slap to the face. Undeterred, the Time Lord revealed: "You have no idea how good that feels!" (Though it's unclear whether he was talking about the kiss or the slap…)

Captain Jack Harkness

Now this really was just a quickie! Ole Jack was not backward in coming forward about his admiration for the Ninth Doctor, even wanting to "dance" with him after their initial meeting, but he finally plucked up the courage for a kiss shortly before the time agent was to meet his doom at the plungers of the Daleks in "The Parting of the Ways" (2005). Jack gets extra points for also placing both hands on the Doctor's face. Nice technique, Harkness!

Donna Noble

2008's "The Unicorn and the Wasp" saw the bubbly Miss Noble take her time before puckering up and sharing a smooch with the Tenth Doctor, but when she did, boy-oh-boy, she kissed like no other! Granted, she was trying to shock her best friend so that the cyanide that had recently been placed in his drink (and drank) was detoxed out of his body. Dunno why a kiss from Chiswick's finest was such a shock for the Gallifreyan, especially after he wanted "to mate" with her.

Dr. Grace Holloway

What a difference a regeneration makes! As soon as he was the handsome, younger, and hairier Eighth Doctor (apologies to the Seventh Doctor), the Gallifreyan planted his lips on the first woman who came his way in the 1996 TV movie. Oddly, she had just killed him. One wonders what the Time Lord would have done had she actually saved his life.

Idris

Whilst technically not the Doctor's *actual* wife (she's somewhere else here), the human embodiment of the TARDIS did factually plant the odd kiss or two on her inside traveler. After her first try in "The Doctor's Wife" (2011), the doolally one tried a more aggressive tactic, and sank her teeth into the Time Lord. "Biting's excellent. It's like kissing, only there's a winner!" she exclaimed to the Doctor's bemusement. Though they would hit it off eventually, sadly, we never discovered what her "new idea" about kissing was.

Madame de Pompadour

Now this was a proper smooch-arama! Tongues and everything! In relative terms, the Tenth Doctor had just met the French girl, but Reinette Poisson had known of her strange visitor for many years. Upon his return into her life, the future Queen wasted no time in backing him against a wall for a smooch the Gallifreyan seemed to rather enjoy in "The Girl in the Fireplace" (2006). Laughing uproariously, he realized, "I just snogged Madame de Pompadour!" Sadly, the laughs soon turned to tears.

Rose

Ah, lovely Rose. She managed a few kisseroos with her much older buddy during her time in the TARDIS (and with more than one Doctor!). I shan't go into them all but who could forget her lustful grab at the Tenth Doctor in 2006's "New Earth" whilst she was "possessed" by bitchy human trampoline Cassandra (so she said), or her saliva-filled encounter on Bad Wolf Bay (granted, with the Meta-Crisis Doctor) in "Journey's End" (2008). My personal favorite, however, was with the Ninth Doctor in "The Parting of the Ways" (2005). "My head. It's killing me," the former shopgirl purred. Old Niney dropped his Northern front and puckered up with, "I think you need a Doctor." The old smoothie!

River Song

Ah, so many kisses, so many different meanings. Sometimes sad, sometimes happy, and sometimes just damn nasty! Check out River (even before she was really River) just after she regenerated in "Let's

Kill Hitler" (2011), where she poisoned the Eleventh Doctor. Bad girl! Thankfully, for him (and the rest of the universe), his future wife repented and kissed him again, subbing him the rest of her regenerations. Their time together included a number of smooches but none more so heartbreaking than in his TARDIS tomb on Trenzalore in "The Name of the Doctor" (2013). "You are always here to me. And I always listen, and I can always see you," he pined shortly before entering his own time stream to save Clara. His seemingly final kiss to his wife may have been an echo, but it sure felt real.

Joan Redfern

More heartbreak, as the Tenth Doctor discovered when he became the human John Smith, was in order to evade the Family of Blood in 2007's "Human Nature"/"The Family of Blood." As a teacher, he fell for Joan Redfern, the school's nurse, and the two enjoyed the odd snog in his room (won't someone please think of the children!). In a glimpse of what their future might be together, the couple certainly got down to more than just kissing, but it wasn't to be as he returned to his former Time Lord self. What could have been…

13 Non-Dalek Stories Featuring Daleks

Title clear enough? No? Ok. This list is a collection of tales that feature Skaro's finest, but are not actually "Dalek" stories. Got that? (We've tried to avoid flashbacks using previously used footage, incidentally.)

I. "The Space Museum" (1965)

Not even two years after their very first appearance and the Daleks are already getting mocked—and in their own show! Slipping himself inside one, William Hartnell takes much glee in parading around in the bump-laden travel machine in the titular museum.

2. "The War Games" (1969)

A blink-and-you'll-miss-it turn as a solitary Dalek appears on the "thought channel" opened up between the Second Doctor and the Time Lords.

3. "Frontier in Space" (1973)

Perhaps it's slightly contentious to include this episode, as you could argue that "Frontier in Space" forms a larger story with its follow-up, "Planet of the Daleks." But "Frontier" is more about Ogrons and Draconians. Plus, the Daleks didn't appear until the last moments of this story (the final third of the sixth installment). And what a shock it was—not as shocking as Pertwee's Dalek impersonation, though.

4. "The Five Doctors" (1983)

Despite a prominent position on the VHS cover (the second version, for fact fans), the 20th Anniversary story features only one Dalek. And a not very good one at that. After tooling around the immensely shiny corridors in some building on Gallifrey, the marauding trash can gets defeated by an elderly man (supposedly the Doctor, but I guess we'll never really know) and his raincoat-wearing, heavily made-up granddaughter.

5. "Doctor Who" (1996)

For some reason, known only to the creators of the 1996 "event," the Master was exterminated on Skaro by the Daleks. Though not seen, we do hear a rather Smurfy version of their familiar maniacal trill as they exterminate the renegade Time Lord. Curiously, early production artwork showed that the pepperpots were to make a more substantial, and more spidery, appearance.

6. "The Next Doctor" (2008)

Not quite an appearance from Skaro's finest here, but Dalek technology. And in a Cybermen story, no less! Must be a real kick in the Cyberteeth for them to have to steal their enemy's gadget ("The Dimension Vault") to fulfill their plan.

7. "The Waters of Mars" (2009)

Clever, clever Daleks. Even they recognize a fixed point in time (unlike some of the show's writers). Little Adelaide Brooke came face to face with one in a rather typically beautiful Russell T. Davies scene, during flashback to the events of "The Stolen Earth"/"Journey's End."

8. "The End of Time" Part Two (2010)

While we don't get a look at any actual Daleks, we do witness their pummeled fleet in the ruins of Gallifrey—so we must assume some of them were wandering around.

9. "The Beast Below" (2010)

Thankfully, some much-needed drama and interest were injected into this 2010 tale (even Moffat isn't too enamored with it) with the surprise reveal that Churchill has the shadow of a Dalek in his office. However, like "Frontier in Space," it merely acted as a prelude to a proper Dalek story.

10. "The Pandorica Opens"/"The Big Bang" (2010)

A double dose of Skarosian action in the Series 5 finale with shiny new bigger Daleks in the first part and then a stone Dalek in the closing half. The latter got all upset and emotional upon meeting River Song for some reason.

11. "The Wedding of River Song" (2011)

Another very brief appearance here with the Eleventh Doctor tracking one down and looking worse for wear.

12. "The Day of the Doctor" (2013)

Perhaps another contentious entry, as you could call it a Dalek story. For these purposes, let's call the 50th Anniversary special a Doctor vs. Doctor story. Regardless, there's a lot of the little guys on show here, and all up to no good!

13. "The Time of the Doctor" (2013)

Matt Smith's final story saw a sixth appearance from the Daleks as he battled them (along with many other familiar foes) on the fields of Trenzalore.

16 Underappreciated Classic *Doctor Who* Stories

Doctor Who fans can be an odd bunch at times (and by that, I mean, all the time)—what's gold to one is dross to another. And when you think everyone is agreed on a genuine stinker ("Timelash," for example), you'll find it has admirers in abundance. But here are—in no particular order—some of the stories that for whatever reason, get overlooked, underseen, and, perhaps, undervalued.

"The Awakening" (1984)

Two-parters are often forgotten (in classic *Doctor Who*, at any rate). This Peter Davison story, while perhaps best known to *Who* fans for a famous blooper featuring a horse, has some tremendous imagery and beautiful locations. Best of all is the villain of the piece, the Malus, who put the willies right up me as a young boy. Its appearance in the TARDIS as an almost monkey-like being is unsettling, while its full appearance featuring a giant head may remind older readers of the arcade game Sinistar (which also scared me as a youngster).

"The Ambassadors of Death" (1970)

I suspect, since the DVD of this story was released last year, that this Jon Pertwee seven-parter (yes, you read correctly—seven) is currently being reassessed by fans. There's a tremendous energy throughout (okay, perhaps a couple of episodes could have been snipped) but its change of locale and story twists are more than enough to make this a hugely pleasing outing. Best of all are the cliffhangers (there are some crackers in "The Ambassadors of Death"), which find the famous *Doctor Who* sting acutely breaking in on the action with a fraction of a second to spare. Very modern and very exciting. The use and placement of in-episode stings to punctuate the start-of-episode recap are also to be highly commended for their ingenuity.

"The Leisure Hive" (1980)

Kicking off the eighties in measurable style, and by that I mean, glitzy, this Tom Baker four-parter saw the beginning of the end for his time in the TARDIS. The Argolins were straight out of a David Bowie video but the Foamasi were an interesting and excellently designed alien (despite their realization not being quite so excellent). Highlights include seeing Baker getting his limbs ripped apart and an expertly executed aged Doctor, a top makeup job. It was a fresh start for the decade and a signpost of things to come.

"The Ark" (1966)

Detractors of this William Hartnell outing often cite the Monoids and invisible Refusians but any story that features the line "Take them to the security kitchen!" needs to be appreciated. In all seriousness, "The Ark" is notable, and well worth watching for a few reasons: the interference that the Doctor and his companions have unwittingly caused (bringing the common cold into contact with an alien race); the results of this action many years down the line when the TARDIS returns to the same spot; and a cracking, visually beautiful cliffhanger to its second episode.

"Black Orchid" (1982)

Another two-parter and another story set in the past for Peter Davison and his young gang. Its brevity serves the story perfectly in this Agatha Christie–esque tale with a dark and horrific family secret at its heart. The location shooting is a joy, not to mention tremendously English, and the costumes are a blast—though the Doctor's harlequin outfit is deeply unsettling with its eerie mask and deceptively colorful facade. Also worth noting is the terrific cast, featuring Michael Cochrane (recently seen as Reverend Travis in *Downton Abbey*), Barbara Murray (*Passport to Pimlico*), and Moray Watson (*Rumpole of the Bailey*), as well as that incredibly moving denouement.

"The Greatest Show in the Galaxy" (1988–89)

Clowns! Killer clowns! Argh! some of you may be saying. While certainly not underappreciated by Sylvester McCoy fans (all twelve of them), those who are less impressed with the Seventh Doctor's run will find much to enjoy in this four-parter. Apart from the meta-inclusion of Gian Sammarco (television's original Adrian Mole) as Whizz Kid—a thinly veiled parody of the *Doctor Who* fan (nice prophetic bow tie, though), the highlight is most definitely Ian Reddington's role as Chief Clown. A superb performance and, still to this day, one of *Who*'s finest villains.

"The Android Invasion" (1975)

Often overlooked due to its placing in the legendary Season 13, where every story is a classic and sandwiched between fan-favorites "Pyramids of Mars" and "The Brain of Morbius," this Tom Baker and Elisabeth Sladen four-parter has much going for it, and very little against. The Kraals are a fantastically designed monster and their simple Earth invasion is refreshing. But it's their titular androids that make for such a haunting viewing. Witness as Sarah Jane Smith's face falls off to reveal the ghostly circuitry beneath. *shudder* Again, the location shooting serves the story well, with some stunning village shots (the Doctor tied to a cross) and the opening "death" of a UNIT soldier. It's the very essence of classic Who, from Who legend and "creator" of the Daleks Terry Nation.

"The Mind of Evil" (1971)

Like previous entry "The Ambassadors of Death," I suspect this six-parter will be reassessed on its recent release on DVD, now restored to full color. And what a cracker this is. Despite being a six-parter, "The Mind of Evil" keeps its pace and interest maintained throughout. While not quite gritty, prison scenes add to the chaotic nature of the tale and there's yet another delicious appearance from Roger Delgado as renegade Time Lord, the Master.

"Frontios" (1984)

For us, this is a genuine classic, and it perturbs us somewhat that there are fans out there who dislike this Peter Davison tale so much. (But such is the life of a Doctor Who fan…we accept this). I mean, it's got the TARDIS BREAKING UP INTO PIECES!!! That should surely be enough, but there's more. "Monsters" of the piece, the Tractators, while not perfect on screen, are one of Doctor Who's most interesting additions—think giant woodlice that suck people into the ground. It's a proper horror story in the guise of a science-fiction tale, a trope that Doctor Who does all too well.

"Terror of the Vervoids" (1986)

More Agatha Christie–style fun here as the Sixth Doctor embarked on his own Murder on the Orient Express (someone is even seen reading the book in the story). It's a solid tale, and if you removed the frankly tedious "Trial of a Time Lord" moments from it, you'd be left with a cracking Who story with a damn threatening monster, the Vervoids. Of course, there's more than meets the eye to these guys and their needs, but I shan't spoil that for you.

Doctor Who (The 1996 Paul McGann TV Movie)

One of my biggest gripes for the Eighth Doctor's one-night stand in the middle of the nineties is its name. We all just call it "The 1996 Paul McGann TV Movie" rather than its proper, and rather useless, name, Doctor Who. Anyway, title grumbles aside, the only on-screen appearance of Paul McGann as everyone's favorite Gallifreyan (to date) does have much in its favor (despite an ending that not only makes little sense, it actively pisses on the show's history and the very notion of what it means to be a time traveler)—namely Paul McGann. The

Withnail & I actor puts in such a wonderfully Doctor-y performance that it would ensure a career in audio and books for years to come.

"Nightmare of Eden" (1979)

What this extraordinary Tom Baker four-parter lacks in production values and acting, it makes up for in ideas and barminess. The Mandrels, the "monsters" of the piece, may well have looked and acted like they stepped out of *The Muppet Show*, but this is a gritty tale of drug-running on an intergalactic scale. The Fourth Doctor is appalled as he gets embroiled in what he genuinely believes to be an evil but by the time we hear him bellow, "My fingers, my arms, my legs, my everything!" any notion of gravity has somewhat dissipated. It was a story, we should say, that utterly terrified us as children and, if you can get over the performances—which, we have to admit, are gruesomely hilarious—and the production (poor, at best), then there's much to admire. We suspect, however, there's now more to have a giggle at than think about.

"The Pirate Planet" (1978)

As the second story in the infamous "Key to Time" season, this story from Douglas Adams (the man behind the *Hitchhikers Guide to the Galaxy*, as if you didn't know) is positively bristling with ideas. The planet in question is hollow and has been materializing around other planets, mining their resources and leaving tiny remains all in a bid to attain immortality. Best of all is Tom Baker's face-off with the Pirate Captain, a Darth Vader–esque man/machine hybrid—"Appreciate it…appreciate it! You commit mass destruction and murder on a scale that's almost inconceivable and you ask me to appreciate it!" the Doctor questions in disbelief. Brilliant stuff from Baker. As you'd expect from Adams, there's humor and high concepts galore.

"Mawdryn Undead" (1983)

Talk about timey-wimey! The Fifth Doctor was getting up to all sorts of flim-flammery back in the seventies/eighties in this four-parter which acts as a sequel of sorts to the "Key to Time" season mentioned above. For its time, and even re-watching now, "Mawdryn Undead" is an extremely fast-paced piece which darts between two time zones in the most pleasing, and modern, of fashions. Despite the UNIT dating controversy (using the Brigadier as teacher in the eighties), fans can revel in the fake Doctor, the titular Mawdryn (who's traveling with his chums through eternity doomed to a life of perpetual death) who tries to convince Tegan and Sarah that he has merely regenerated. Design-wise, it's a triumph with a beautiful ship, super brain-bulging aliens, and a haunting score from Paddy Kingsland.

"Invasion of the Dinosaurs" (1974)

Another story often put to the side due to the main monsters of the tale, the dinosaurs. Yes, they are bloody terrible. Laughably so. I shan't disabuse you of that notion—there's absolutely nothing positive to say about them at all, from design to execution. But it's the story in this Jon Pertwee six-parter that's worth the re-evaluation. Someone is tampering with time and using the prehistoric baddies to evacuate London, all in the noble cause of the environment and the future of mankind. In an exciting twist, trusty old Mike Yates turns out to be a traitor (believing he is in the right), adding to the layers of this intriguing tale. "Invasion of the Dinosaurs" is worth watching for the opening episode alone, with its eerie empty streets and unfolding mystery, classic *Who*.

"The Five Doctors" (1983)

There are very few *Doctor Who* stories I can just stick on and watch at any point, regardless of mood—and this 20th Anniversary special is one of them. In fact, it's probably the *Doctor Who* story I've watched the most over the years, never tiring of the multi-Doctor fun. Some "fans," and I use the term quite wrongly, are sniffy about this and often ignore it, possibly because it's such a joyous affair. But what should be remembered is the fact that aside from the sheer delight of seeing five Doctors together on-screen (well, okay, three), the notion of searching for immortality is fascinating, especially when there are corrupt Time Lords sniffing around. Best of all, for me, is the Raston Warrior Robot—when are we gonna see that guy again?

Alternate Universes

It's not enough for the Doctor to travel through time and space. Oh no, he has to delve into the murky and mysterious depths of parallel worlds, divergent time lines, and alternate universes. Here are those moments.

Inferno" (1970)

This Jon Pertwee classic is the daddy of parallel universe stories. After some experimental drilling, some green ooze, and a faulty TARDIS, the Third Doctor was transported to a different UK under a fascist regime. There, he encountered a very different version of the Brigadier and his UNIT chums.

"Father's Day" (2005)

Due to Rose Tyler's selfishness, 1987 Earth was thrown into the clutches of the Reapers. When she stopped her father, Pete Tyler, dying in a car accident, an alternate world was created, thus allowing the time-eating monsters in. Things got so bad that even the Doctor was taken—but Pete's self-sacrifice righted the time line. Though it wasn't the last we heard of him…

"Rise of the Cybermen"/"The Age of Steel" (2006)

Mickey keenly observes "an alternative to our world where everything's the same but a little bit different, like, I don't know, traffic lights are blue, Tony Blair never got elected." Pete's World was uncannily similar to Earth and proved to be an emotional environment for both Mickey and Rose as they encountered deceased loved ones.

Of Course, We Didn't Forget…

Here are some more stories that include glimpses into possible futures:

- **"The Space Museum"** (1965)
- **"Day of the Daleks"** (1972)
- **"Pyramids of Mars"** (1975)
- **"The Hungry Earth"/"Cold Blood"** (2010)
- **"The Girl Who Waited"** (2011)
- **"Journey to the Centre of the TARDIS"** (2013)

"Last of the Time Lords" (2007)

It was called "The Year That Never Was" when Time Lord renegade the Master used the Paradox Machine, by bastardizing the Doctor's TARDIS, to create his own, new time line. For a whole year, the black-suited rogue ruled Earth, only to be brought down by Martha Jones and one word: "Doctor."

"Forest of the Dead" (2008)

Poor Donna Noble managed to create a whole new universe for herself upon leaving the Library. In it, she met the man of her dreams and had a family.

"Turn Left" (2008)

If "Inferno" was the daddy, then this is the mother of parallel universe stories. Donna Noble visited a fortune-teller on the planet Shan Shen. Little did she know that this fortune-teller was part of the Trickster's Brigade and used a Time Beetle (possibly called "Ringo") to change the Chiswick temp's past, thus creating a new reality where the Tenth Doctor died saving Earth from the Racnoss. The resulting events were chaotic and heartbreaking, though Donna saved the universe. Again.

"The Wedding of River Song" (2011)

In this time line, it was always 5:02 pm on April 22, 2011. And all because the Eleventh Doctor messed around with a fixed point in time. This alternate London looked pretty groovy, with Charles Dickens promoting his new work, pterodactyls flying around, and Roman chariots parading the streets. Through marriage, however, this anomaly was fixed.

50 Years of Firsts

Well, not quite fifty. For some reason, the BBC thought it was a good idea not to screen *Doctor Who* for a number of years. But below you can check off a first for every year of the world's greatest TV show.

1963	First Episode! ("An Unearthly Child")
1964	First companion to leave ("The Dalek Invasion of Earth")
1965	First movie (*Dr Who & the Daleks*)
1966	First regeneration ("The Tenth Planet")
1967	First time the Doctor's face appeared in the title sequence ("The Macra Terror")
1968	First appearance of the sonic screwdriver ("Fury from the Deep")
1969	First time we see the Doctor's home planet ("The War Games")
1970	First episode in color ("Spearhead from Space")
1971	First appearance of the Master ("Terror of the Autons")
1972	First multi-Doctor story ("The Three Doctors")
1973	First mention of Gallifrey ("The Time Warrior")
1974	First use of regeneration to describe the process ("Planet of the Spiders")
1975	First appearance of Davros ("Genesis of the Daleks")
1976	First mention of the twelve regenerations limit ("The Deadly Assassin")
1977	First K9 story ("The Invisible Enemy")
1978	First full season-long story arc ("The Key to Time")
1979	First story filmed abroad ("City of Death")
1980	First unfinished story ("Shada")
1981	First use of the Cloister Bell ("Logopolis")
1982	First death of a regular companion ("Earthshock")

1983	First appearance of Rassilon ("The Five Doctors")
1984	First time the Doctor strangled a companion ("The Twin Dilemma")
1985	First time the Doctor's TARDIS chameleon circuit worked ("Attack of the Cybermen")
1986	First hiatus (Boo!)
1987	First spoon playing ("Time and the Rani")
1988	First on-screen Dalek going upstairs ("Remembrance of the Daleks")
1989	First *Star Wars* reference ("Survival")

1996	First time the Doctor revealed he was "half-human" (*Doctor Who: TV Movie*)
2005	First mention of the Time War ("Rose")
2006	First time the Doctor said he was a dad ("Fear Her")
2007	First use of "timey-wimey wibbly-wobbly" ("Blink")
2008	First time we see the Doctor get a daughter ("The Doctor's Daughter")
2009	First episode filmed in HD ("Planet of the Dead")
2010	First time the Doctor head-butts someone ("The Lodger")
2011	First time a dartboard is seen in the TARDIS ("The Rebel Flesh")
2012	First use of a Nintendo Wii ("The Power of Three")
2013	First time we see future regeneration of the Doctor ("The Day of the Doctor")
2014	First female Master ("Dark Water")

Doctor Braveheart

Doctor Who has quite the relationship with Scotland. Sylvester McCoy, David Tennant, and Peter Capaldi are all Scots, as is current head writer Steven Moffat. Yet, the country's presence in *Who* has been slim with very few visits north of the border. Here are those rare moments.

"Deep Breath" (2014)

Instead of returning Clara home at the end of their first adventure together, the Doctor managed to stop off in Glasgow (where his new persona would fit in, according to his companion); a trick he'll pull off again in this list with another companion. Although, it has to be said, the Scottish city does look an awful lot like Cardiff.

"The Hand of Fear" (1976)

Though we didn't know it at the time, and had to wait until 2006's "School Reunion" to discover this fact, companion Sarah Jane Smith was actually dropped off in Aberdeen, and not Croydon as requested.

"Terror of the Zygons" (1975)

Though the crew never set foot in Scotland, this spectacularly good Fourth Doctor four-parter makes for a very believable Scottish environment, even despite the use of bagpipes. The origin of the Loch Ness Monster is revealed in the Zygons story—the mighty Skarasen, a huge beast that terrified the inhabitants of Tulloch Moor (near Loch Ness, according to the story but, in actual fact, the real Tulloch Moor is not so close.)

"Tooth and Claw" (2006)

"Are we in Scotland?" cooed the Tenth Doctor in a Scottish accent (not bad work there from Paisley-born David Tennant), as he met Queen Victoria on her way to Balmoral (which isn't too far from the aforementioned Aberdeen). This werewolf adventure was set entirely in Scotland, though, of course, shot entirely in Wales. Top marks to Billie Piper for her Scottish "accent" and for the use of "timorous beastie"—a tribute to the poet Rabbie Burns.

"Timelash" (1985)

Some would rather choose to forget this Sixth Doctor story but it does feature H.G. Wells, the father of science fiction. With his companion, Peri, they picked up the writer in the Highlands close to Inverness, while the evil Borad was timelashed to the twelfth century, where it would become the Loch Ness Monster (somewhat going against the events of "Terror of the Zygons," above.)

"The Highlanders" (1966)

The Second Doctor, along with Ben and Polly, arrived in Scotland just after the Battle of Culloden (go and ask your teachers about that one, kids!) where the Time Lord befriended a bunch of Jacobites. Here he would form a strong and lasting relationship with kilt-loving Jamie McCrimmon. And yet another story with an Inverness connection (a jail for prisoners was situated there).

"The Name of the Doctor" (2013)

Good old Sontaran Strax liked a fight, and where better to go for a quality bash than Glasgow, home of the head-butt (affectionately known as a "Glasgow Kiss"). Perhaps this was an amusing dig at former Glaswegian Steven Moffat who penned the tale. Either way, the city hasn't changed much since Victorian times.

Top 10 Scary Houses

During his time traveling the universe, the Doctor has encountered his fair share of creepy houses. From stately homes to ordinary flats, all have had their sinister edge.

10. Paradise Towers in "Paradise Towers" (1987)

What's scarier than one creepy house? Answer: a whole block of them in this Sylvester McCoy adventure from 1987. Accompanied by Mel, played by screaming ginger Bonnie Langford, the Seventh Doctor faced roving gangs, broken lifts, wonky waste disposal units, crumpet-loving old ladies, and, worst of all, eighties production values.

9. Haunted House in "The Chase" (1965)

Too obvious? An actual haunted house? When the First Doctor and his chums came across this abode in episode four of "The Chase," they were surprised to find Frankenstein's monster and Dracula together. While the Doctor felt it didn't actually exist with its stereo-typical "creaking doors, thunder and lightning, monsters," suggesting they were in a "world of dreams," companion Ian was closest when he suspected a simpler explanation was behind it all. The gang didn't spot the sign, proclaiming, "Festival of Ghana 1996, cancelled by Peking, Frankenstein's House of Horrors, price $10."

8. Council Block in "Night Terrors" (2011)

Like number ten here, this council block was terrifying for numerous reasons, though the fact that it harbored a slightly unstable alien was per-haps the most frightening. In real life, it's Dyrham House in Bristol, should you fancy a visit. Of course, there's another even scarier place in "Night Terrors"—the Dollhouse! With its very creepy peg dolls… *shiver*

7. The Gateway in "Warriors' Gate" (1981)

Not really a house this one, granted, but it's an unnerving place none-theless. Stuck in E-Space (yes, between D- and F-Space), Tom Baker said good-bye to his wife, Lalla Ward, and K9 here, who weren't put off by the faceless guard and crazy universe-hopping mirror.

6. 1980s Hotel in "The God Complex" (2011)

Did someone say *The Shining*? Oddly, the Doctor reckons it's an eight-ies hotel, yet it has a distinct seventies vibe about it. Regardless of decade, the building (which was, in fact, computer generated), scared the life out of those who visited. Rita, a Muslim, suggested it was Jah-annam, the Islamic concept of Hell. Whatever it meant to its various

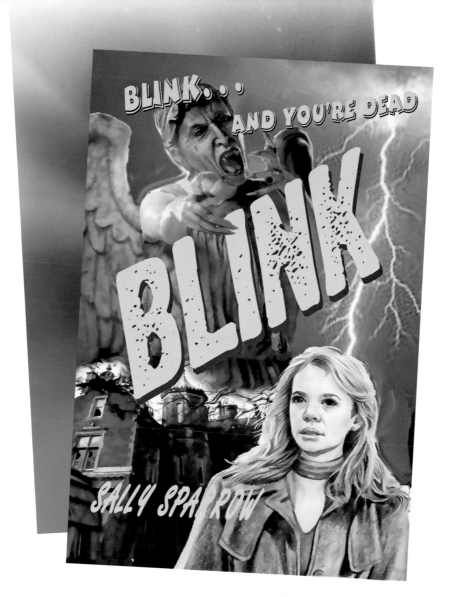

occupants, each room had something different awaiting them. Matt Smith once revealed at a convention that Room 11 contained eleven silhouettes being hung. Cheery guy.

5. Gabriel Chase in "Ghost Light" (1989)

Back to the actual eighties now with a proper scary house, this time in the form of Gabriel Chase, a mansion Perivale visited by Seventh Doctor Sylvester McCoy and his companion, Sophie Aldred. The duo visited in 1883 when it was a rural hamlet of Perivale, before it was more familiar to companion Ace in 1983, when it was part of London. If you want to see it for yourself, take a trip to Stanton Court in Weymouth, Dorset, for some sinister times.

4. Cranleigh Hall in "Black Orchid" (1982)

Secrets hidden in another mansion. And there's nothing quite as juicy as an English family secret. The Fifth Doctor was mistaken for a killer as he and his friends danced, drank, and ate, all at the hospitality of Lord Cranleigh. But what was hiding in the rooms? Creeping through secret corridors? Hiding behind a mask…?

3. Caliburn House in "Hide" (2013)

Professor Alec Palmer and his assistant, Emma Grayling, went ghost-busting here in 1974, looking for the Witch of the Well. And Caliburn House did seem to scare the Eleventh Doctor and Clara, both sharing the odd scream in a Scooby Doo–like way. Fact fans may note that this story is set when Jon Pertwee's final story, "Planet of the Spiders" (1974), was broadcast.

2. Scarman's Mansion in "Pyramids of Mars" (1975)

Speaking of facts, the reality behind the home used in this classic Egyptian-tinged Tom Baker tale are fascinating. Also used in another Fourth Doctor adventure (1977's "Image of the Fendahl"), Stargroves, in Hampshire, is a manor house once used by the Rolling Stones to record their brand of "devil's music." But even *more* interesting is the fact that Lord Carnavorn was once its "Lord of the Manor," a man who uncovered the tomb of one of the most famous Egyptians of them all, Tutankhamun. Spooky, huh?

1. Wester Drumlins House in "Blink" (2007)

Even without the intervention of the Weeping Angels, this home is surely the most sinister and freaky of all the houses encountered in *Doctor Who*. Creepiest of all is the fact that the building is actually someone's home. Fields House, a listed building in Newport, Wales, currently has human beings living there. I'm guessing they haven't watched this episode, because if they had, there's no way they'd be living there. Right?

Dino Time!

Everyone loves dinosaurs, right? And in *Doctor Who*, Earth's oldest monsters get the occasional outing and mention. Find every one of those incidents from the show's history here.

"Deep Breath" (2014)

The most recent outing for dinosaurs in *Doctor Who* came in the Twelfth Doctor's first story—in the very first scene! Having gone back to prehistoric times with Clara immediately after his regeneration, the Time Lord befriended a female Tyrannosaurus rex—a dinosaur that wasn't too keen on the taste of the TARDIS, though was referred to as "my lady friend" by the Gallifreyan. Naughty boy.

"Dinosaurs on a Spaceship" (2012)

Pterodactyls again, as well as Velociraptors and a golf-ball loving Triceratops (affectionately dubbed "Tricey" by the Time Lord), were confronted as the Eleventh Doctor and his team (consisting of Amy, Rory, Brian, Queen Nefertiti, and Riddell) make their way around the Silurian Ark (more from them later).

"The Wedding of River Song" (2011)

Check out the sign "Pterodactyls are vermin. Do not feed," as a number of them fly around an alternate London.

"The Big Bang" (2010)

The National Museum visited by Amelia Pond featured dino skeletons as well as, according to their brochure, dinosaurs "on ice."

"The Runaway Bride" (2006)

Donna Noble suggested, much to the Tenth Doctor's surprise, that the Racnoss were tunneling down to the center of the Earth to find dinosaurs.

"Mark of the Rani" (1985)

The Rani, another renegade Time Lord like the Master (who also appears in this story), kept preserved Tyrannosaurus rex embryos in this Sixth Doctor adventure. A biochemist, she was conducting brain experiments on humans, but found herself on the receiving end of her own folly when the Doctor left her with a rapidly growing T. rex to contend with in her TARDIS. She returned for the sequel, "Time and the Rani" (1987), where the nasty Gallifreyan claimed the "potential of the dinosaurs was never fully realized."

"Earthshock" (1982)

No sign of any dinosaurs in this one, though you'll see plenty of fossilized remains in the background. Thanks to the Cybermen and companion Adric, the dinosaurs were wiped out.

"Invasion of the Dinosaurs" (1974)

The Third Doctor and Sarah Jane Smith found a deserted London, populated with the odd dinosaur, including a Tyrannosaurus rex, a Stegosaurus, a Brontosaurus, and a Pterodactyl. Sarah Jane mentioned this story when she met Rose in "School Reunion" (2006).

"Doctor Who and the Silurians" (1970)

While exploring some caves in his second adventure, the Third Doctor came face to face with "some kind of dinosaur," one he couldn't identify. It would appear later again, as plaything of the Silurians.

"The Underwater Menace" (1967)

Though we don't see any, when the Second Doctor lands the TARDIS, he was hoping there would be "prehistoric monsters" outside. (Unfortunately for him, there were none.)

Honorable Mention

"The Wedding of Sarah Jane Smith"

(a 2009 *The Sarah Jane Adventures* story): Upon entering the TARDIS, Clyde Langer asks if he can visit the dinosaurs. (The two-parter starred David Tennant as the Tenth Doctor.)

Doctor Who?

From time to time, the phrase "Doctor Who" is actually used in the show. Sometimes as his name—yes, you read that correctly—and sometimes as a neat in-joke. And sometimes, there's a more mysterious use behind its appearance. Interestingly, the new series has used "Doctor Who" twice as much as the classic run from 1963 to 1989. In fact, the Steven Moffat era has seen more uses of it than anywhere else.

"An Unearthly Child" (1963)

Right from the very first episode, the writers acknowledged the show's title. The First Doctor himself questions Ian with "Doctor who?—what's he talking about?" after being referred to as Doctor Foreman (apparently an addition from William Hartnell). And the aforementioned Ian gets in on the action with "Who is he? Doctor who? Perhaps if we knew his name we might have a clue to all this," after his future wife, Barbara, also refers to the stranger as Doctor Foreman.

"The War Machines" (1966)

Now this *is* a doozy. Crazy computer WOTAN (Will Operating Thought ANalogue) explicitly refers to this, saying on four occasions, "Doctor Who is required." His creator, Professor Brett also uses "Doctor Who" as the Doctor's name twice. Who to believe?

"The Gunfighters" (1966)

A jokey one here as the Doctor finds himself on holiday, with a bad tooth, in the Wild West. When introducing himself as Doctor Caligari (a reference to the 1920 German horror film), he's asked, "Doctor Who?" To which the Doctor replies, "Yes, quite right."

"The Highlanders" (1966)

The Second Doctor was just as mischievous. After introducing himself as "Doktor von Wer" (which translates roughly as "Doctor of Who"), he's queried, Doctor who?" The Doctor replies with, "That's what I said." Cheeky blighter.

"The Curse of Peladon" (1972)

Toward the end of this Jon Pertwee four-parter, after the Doctor has posed as an Earth delegate throughout his time on Peladon, the actual Earth delegate appears. Upon learning of this "Doctor," she asks, "Doctor? What Doctor? Doctor who?" Thankfully, the Doctor and Jo Grant slip away without anyone noticing.

"Black Orchid" (1982)

Oddly, given his frivolity, Fourth Doctor Tom Baker didn't get to share his predecessor's fun, and it's not until we reach the Fifth Doctor, in his first season, that he's asked by Lady Cranleigh, "How do you do? Doctor…who?" Peter Davison remained incognito on his identity.

"Silver Nemesis" (1988)

Slightly less playful than previous mentions, Lady Peinforte is more confrontational in this 1988 Cybermen adventure. Speaking with Ace, she questions, "Doctor who? Have you never wondered where he came from, who he is?" Later in the story, the companion would unequivocally demand of Sylvester McCoy's Time Lord, "Doctor? Who are you?" (Ever the wag, he didn't answer.)

"Rose" (2005)

Not a spoken mention here but visible on the soon-to-be-dead Clive's computer screen. When visiting the Internerd's shed, Rose finds evidence of the Doctor's life on Earth before their meeting. Accompanying an image of Christopher Eccleston's Doctor are the words "Doctor Who? Have you seen this man?" Poor Clive.

"The Empty Child" (2005)

Not long after, Rose introduces the Ninth Doctor as Mr. Spock to Captain Jack Harkness, about which the Time Lord is slightly bewildered. Rose counters with, "What was I supposed to say? You don't have a name! Don't you ever get tired of Doctor? Doctor who?"

"Boom Town" (2005)

Nice and quick: when making a surprise visit to Cardiff's Mayor (who was a Slitheen), Gallifrey's finest says to the secretary, "Tell her the Doctor would like to see her." And, guess what, she asks, "Doctor who?"

"The Christmas Invasion" (2005)

On to the David Tennant era now and it's Jackie Tyler who questions the identity of this new mysterious stranger: "What d'you mean, 'That's the Doctor'? Doctor who?" Cue titles!

"The Girl in the Fireplace" (2006)

As mysterious as she was lovely, the doomed Madame de Pompadour enters the Doctor's mind and searches, "Doctor. Doctor who? It's more than just a secret, isn't it?" She never found out, either.

"The Next Doctor" (2008)

Jackson Lake, posing as the Doctor, had his very own companion, too, and she got to ask the immortal question: "Doctor who?" On being told, "Just the Doctor," Rosita claimed, "Well, there can't be two of you!" Pity, as David Morrissey would have made a damn fine Time Lord.

"The Impossible Astronaut" (2011)

Two mentions here in this 2011 opener starring Matt Smith. In the opening seconds, we find Charles II angrily bursting into a room, demanding, "Where's the Doctor?" to which the reply comes from artist Matlida, "Doctor who?" (The naughty and naked Gallifreyan was hiding under her skirt.) Elsewhere, Canton Delaware III asks Amy Pond, "Doctor who, exactly?"

"Let's Kill Hitler" (2011)

After being told by the Teselecta (in the form of Amy) that River Song has killed the Doctor, he has the bare-faced cheek to emerge from the TARDIS, bedecked in a tuxedo and brandishing a cane and then proclaim, "Sorry, did you say she killed the Doctor? The Doctor? Doctor Who?"

"The Wedding of River Song" (2011)

Dorium Maldovar drops the big one in the finale to Series 6: "The first question. The question that must never be answered, hidden in plain sight. The question you've been running from all your life. Doctor who? Doctor who? Doc-tor who!"

"Asylum of the Daleks" (2012)

Speaking of multiple uses of the phrase, this episode features an enormous amount of usage for "Doctor Who." Darla, the Daleks, and their Prime Minister all repeatedly ask, "Doctor Who?" while the Doctor himself dances around the TARDIS chanting the two words. Interestingly, like Dorium, he says it three times.

"The Angels Take Manhattan" (2012)

Not to be outdone, River Song wants a piece of the fun, too. "Weren't you the woman who killed the Doctor?" playfully queries Matt Smith's Time Lord, to which his on-screen wife replies, "Doctor who?" Jeez, get a room.

"The Snowmen" (2012)

Another story with multiple usage here: new girl Clara asks "Doctor who?" of the Doctor twice; Jenny asks it once (when questioned by Clara, "Do you know about him? The Doctor?"); and the Doctor uses it as Punch (from Punch & Judy) shortly before he shatters the Ice Governess with his Sonic.

"The Bells of Saint John" (2013)

Clara, being the greedy girl, gets to say "Doctor who?" (albeit in different modern day persona) a further three times in her first "proper" outing as a companion. Turns out the Doctor enjoys hearing the words said out loud. (And, again, it's said three times.)

"The Name of the Doctor" (2013)

And another threesome here as the Great Intelligence, in the form of Richard E. Grant, asks "Doctor who?" of Strax, Jenny, and Clara while outside the Time Lord's tomb on Trenzalore. Like many before, he never found out (or, if he did, he died before he could pass on this info).

"The Name of the Doctor" (2013)

Aw, poor Handles. The shortest on-screen companion yet, in reality, the longest serving (spending hundreds of years with Matt Smith on Trenzalore). Translating the various life forms nearby, the Cyber head repeats "Doctor who?" many, many times.

"Dark Water" (2014)

Peter Capaldi got the chance to utter the words (ironic as the actor loves to refer to the character as "Doctor Who" as opposed to "the Doctor) in the penultimate story of his first series. The physician in question was the short-lived friend of Missy, Dr. Chang.

Far Out, Man

Past, present, and future—the Doctor, in his many incarnations, loves traveling every time, everywhere. But when did he go as far as he possibly could? Here are the top 10 *Doctor Who* stories set furthest and maybe farthest in the future.

10. "The Long Game" (2005)

Doctor Who's return with Christopher Eccleston at the helm featured a number of adventures set some time in our future (you'll see more soon). This futuristic tale is set in 200000. The downside? It features Adam.

9. "Bad Wolf"/"The Parting of the Ways" (2005)

A sequel, of sorts, to the previous entry. Just one hundred years later in 200100, the Ninth Doctor revisits Satellite 5, now the Games Station, only to find that his good work in "The Long Game" (2005) was not good at all.

8. "The Mysterious Planet" (1986)/"Dragonfire" (1987)

These two very different stories, featuring the Sixth and Seventh Doctors, respectively, both took place in 2000000. The former saw Earth moved by the Time Lords to a new location in the universe, while the latter saw Mel leave the TARDIS and Ace join.

7. "Hide" (2013)

When the Eleventh Doctor was investigating the "ghost" at Caliburn House in 1974, he took a trip to the ends of the Earth, literally (though not quite as far as the next entry). The exact date isn't stated, but I think it's safe to say that it is deserved of this spot in the chart.

6. "The End of the World" (2005)

Just two episodes into the Ninth Doctor's reign and we see the end of our lovely planet in the year 5000000000. This would be the start of the so-called "New Earth" trilogy that continued the following year...

5. "New Earth" (2006)

... and just twenty-three years later (in their time). The newly regenerated Tenth Doctor took Rose on a trip to 5000000023, where he found a message from an old friend but also an old adversary waiting for him, too.

4. "Gridlock" (2007)

Concluding the triumvirate and set in 5000000053, the Tenth Doctor revisited New Earth again, with new companion Martha Jones. The trainee doctor didn't seem that impressed with flying cars and a population almost destroyed by drugs. "Looks like the same old Earth to me, on a Wednesday afternoon," she sighed. Miss Jones was just annoyed that she was being taken to former haunts of her predecessor, Rose.

3. "The Ark" (1966)

Another story where the exact year isn't stated (not on our terms anyway), but in this William Hartnell adventure, the First Doctor claimed they had traveled "at least" ten million years into the future. Rather poetically, they found themselves in the 57th "segment of time," according to one of the last humans on board the titular ship, the Ark.

2. "Frontios" (1984)

Now this one is a bit more interesting. The TARDIS states, "Boundary Error: Time Parameters Exceeded," leading the Fifth Doctor to comment they have "drifted too far into the future."

1. "Utopia" (2007)

Beating them all into a pulp is this tale that saw the return of the Master in the year 100000000000000. Sadly, it also saw the end of the human race as we were transformed into shrunken heads in globes, aka the Toclafane.

Of Course, We Didn't Forget...

There are another two Doctor Who stories where it cannot be identified exactly when they take place. We only know that these adventures are set far in the future:

- **"The Face of Evil"** (1977): no hint given at all apart from the fact that Earth colonists had begun seeking out other planets (so between a little to a lot of time in the future)

- **"The Sun Makers"** (1977): humans have left "Old Earth," but the Doctor states that the planet will be regenerating and suitable for repopulation (so, again, could be a small or a large jump ahead of our time).

Home Is Where the Hearts Are

Oddly, we had to wait over ten years before Gallifrey got an on-screen mention in *Doctor Who* (in 1973's "The Time Warrior"), even though we'd already seen the planet a few times. Collected here are the Doctor's adventures on his home world, which lies in the constellation of Kasterborous.

"The War Games" (1969)

Toward the end of this epic ten-part adventure for the Second Doctor, the Time Lords transported him, accompanied by Jamie and Zoe, back to his "own planet." This story was the first time the phrase "Time Lord" was used to describe the Doctor's people.

"Colony in Space" (1971)

Though not explicitly stated, this Third Doctor take featured a scene between Time Lords discussing perennial bad boy the Master and his use of the Doomsday Weapon.

"The Three Doctors" (1972)

The last story to be set on Gallifrey, without actually stating its name, this romp collected the First, Second, and Third Doctors together as they combined forces with the Time Lords to face an attack by former Gallfreyan hero Omega.

"The Deadly Assassin" (1976)

At the time, many fans were irked by the portrayal of Time Lord society in this exciting Fourth Doctor four-parter set on Gallifrey (the first since its naming mentioned above). "The Deadly Assassin" set the sartorial tone for the rest of the stories here, with high collars and odd headgear.

"The Invasion of Time" (1977)

Just a year after his last sojourn and he was back. Sadly, for the Fourth Doctor, so were the Vardans and the Sontarans, neither of which managed to successfully invade Gallifrey. Or indeed, time. Again, like "The Deadly Assassin," we saw that Time Lord society was a rather corrupt one, with bad eggs all around.

"Arc of Infinity" (1983)

It was the glitzy veneer of the 1980s, and yet the fashion stayed pretty much the same in this Fifth Doctor four-parter. And, as *Doctor Who* was in its 20th Anniversary year, the production team also brought back an old villain, Omega, just ten years after his last outing. Weirdly, one of the guards (a rogue named Maxil) bore quite the resemblance to the Sixth Doctor…

"The Five Doctors" (1983)

More Fifth Doctor fun as he visited his fellow Time Lords on Gallifrey, while his other selves ended up in the Death Zone and then the Tower of Rassilon.

"The Sound of Drums" (2007)

A flashback as we saw the Master face the Untempered Schism on Gallifrey.

"The End of Time" (2010–11)

Rassilon and the gang were up to no good at the end of the Time War, and we were treated to the sights of the Citadel from outside and in. Crumbling away, the Time Lords made a rather bad decision regarding the outcome of their people.

"The Day of the Doctor" (2013)

And in the 50th Anniversary special, Gallifrey was home to 3-D attacks from the Daleks, while the War Council got excited when *all* of the Doctors turned up. Of course, the planet was lost in another universe at the end of the episode, never to be found again. Or was it…?

"Listen" (2014)

Clara visited Gallifrey in this episode and found the young Time Lord above her when she hid under his bed. Sadly, Miss Oswald didn't invite her traveling buddy to join her on his home planet.

Honorable Mention

- **"Gridlock"** (2007): featured the Tenth Doctor reminiscing about Gallifrey, complete with flashback
- **"The Last Day"** (2013), the 50th Anniversary mini-episode: didn't feature any of the Doctors but was set on Gallifrey during the Time War

Not-So-Happy Endings

Doctor Who is known for resolving a situation neatly—enemies vanquished, allies happy. But occasionally, very occasionally, an episode will not have a happy ending. We've avoided stories where companions leave (that has its own section elsewhere in this book).

"The Girl Who Waited" (2011)

Technically, I suppose, this is a companion farewell as we say goodbye to "old" Amy Pond. This shocking ending, with the Eleventh Doctor leaving her to die, showed a different side to both the remaining Amy and her husband, Rory.

"Midnight" (2008)

Just what was that thing? Never named, other than being called the "Midnight Monster," the entity that entered Sky Silvestry and then the Tenth Doctor left as soon as it arrived. With the Time Lord finding himself at the mercy of mob mentality, the uncertainty of the denouement made for an unsettling experience as he revealed his ignorance of the creature. Chills!

"Doctor Who and the Silurians" (1970)

In just his second story on Earth, the Third Doctor discovers that his buddies at UNIT may not be on the same page as him. Upon seeing the destruction of the Silurian base at the hands of the Brigadier and

his chums, the Time Lord complains, "But that's murder. They were intelligent alien beings. A whole race of them. And he's just wiped them out."

"The Girl in the Fireplace" (2006)

Argh, the feels! After just finding love with the lovely Madame de Pompadour, the Tenth Doctor foolishly jumps time only to miss her death. Her untimely demise was mournful, but even sadder was the reveal that the spaceship, which carried the menacing Clockwork Droids, was called the SS *Madame de Pompadour*. A beautiful score from Murray Gold sealed the sadness.

"Vincent and the Doctor" (2010)

This heartbreaking story from Richard Curtis (the man behind films such as 2003's *Love Actually* and 1994's *Four Weddings and a Funeral*) was embroidered with woe after Amy's loss (when Rory "died"). But it was the titular painter Van Gogh who caused this particular unhappy ending. His mental illness was not to be saved by the Doctor, much to Amy's sadness. His work would live on, even if Vincent didn't.

"Warriors of the Deep" (1984)

"There should have been another way," lamented the Fifth Doctor at the end of what was, it has to be said, a pretty bad story. Like his previous encounter with the Silurians, the ending was bleak, with everyone killed, except the Time Lord and his chums. A downbeat debut for Peter Davion's last season as the Galllireyan.

"Cold Blood" (2010)

Amy's beloved Rory died (for the first time), at the hands of Restac, heroically defending the Doctor. Sad as that was, Amy's disappearing memory of her fiancé was even more heartrending.

"The Waters of Mars" (2009)

Crikey, David Tennant goes bad! By becoming the Time Lord Victorious, the Tenth Doctor set about changing time—only to find that time can right itself once more. Having saved Adelaide Brooke from certain death on Mars, it was she who righted time by committing suicide. Bleak doesn't quite cover it.

"Attack of the Cybermen" (1985)

Talk about a bloodbath, 1980s *Doctor Who* had it going on. The Sixth Doctor's arrogance was chipped away as he realized his own error. "It didn't go very well, did it?" he admits to Peri, after the couple managed to survive an encounter with the Cybermen. Perhaps most touchingly, his remorse at his treatment of former bad boy Lytton was revealed: "I don't think I've ever misjudged anybody quite as badly as I did Lytton."

Say Good-bye

With every "Hello!" and "Come aboard!" that's heard in the TARDIS, the Doctor also has to face his hefty share of farewells. Below you'll find some of the most memorable, not to mention heartbreaking, adieus the Time Lord has had to face with his friends and companions.

Amy Pond

But which send-off to choose? Instead of her initial farewell with Rory in their lovely new house (and swanky car), provided so generously by the Eleventh Doctor in "The God Complex" (2011), or her final one in 2013's "The Time of the Doctor" (though that was imaginary), let's look at her tear-filled good-bye with her Raggedy Man in a New York graveyard in "The Angels Take Manhattan" (2012). There, Amy chose to be zapped back in time to join her true love (apparently), Rory, courtesy of a rogue Weeping Angel. I'm sure Pond was upset but the Time Lord seemed deeply affected by this loss and his tears were only consoled by his sometime-wife, River Song.

Romana

"You were the best Romana of them all!" exclaimed the Fourth Doctor as his fellow Gallifreyan chose to stay in E-Space to help the Tharils in "Warrior's Gate" (1981). It was a friendly, smiley affair as one waved to another, even though the Time Lady went on to face the greatest monster of all, without the aid of K9. Though parting in the show, Tom Baker and Lalla Ward stayed together for a short while after in real life, enjoying an eighteen-month marriage.

Susan

Did she jump or was she pushed? Though the Time Lord's granddaughter seemed to protest at being left in twenty-second century London in "The Dalek Invasion of Earth" (1964), Susan did find a genuine bond in human Earth male and freedom fighter, David Campbell. The First Doctor trapped her out of the TARDIS after a particularly nasty encounter with the Daleks, delivering fine lines like, "My dear, your future lies with David and not with a silly old buffer like me," and, "Just go forward in all your beliefs, and prove to me that I am not mistaken in mine." Despite her protestations, the First Doctor sadly proclaimed, "Good-bye, Susan, good-bye, my dear." #sniff.

Ian and Barbara

Not as emotional a good-bye for these two when they left the First Doctor, in comparison to Susan, but the Time Lord did give them a rather sentimental send-off. Like the Gallifreyan's granddaughter, the teachers of Coal Hill left after another meeting with the Daleks, and found themselves back in their own time in London at the denouement of "The Chase" (1965). Using his Time and Space Visualizer, the Doctor watched his friends leave with a smile on his face and remembrance in his heart. Sensing they were being observed, Barbara said, "Good-bye, Doctor! Thanks for the ride!" while Ian added, "It was fun, Doctor! Good-bye!" The final word went to their designated driver: "Yes, I shall miss them, silly old fusspots."

Tegan

A rather unpleasant good-bye for the Australian, and another good-bye after a meeting with the Daleks. Tegan was pretty upset at what she'd just witnessed in "Resurrection of the Daleks" (1984)—a rather high death count (even high for the Time Lord's adventures)—and decided to stay in London, leaving the Fifth Doctor to reflect on his own life choices. Sadly, Tegan instantly regretted her choice and fled back to the TARDIS to rejoin her chums, only to find it dematerializing in her front of her eyes.

Jo Grant

Jeepers, this was a toughie for the Doc. For the first time, the Time Lord seemed genuinely rattled to see a companion leave. In 1973's "The Green Death," Jo decided to settle down with handsome man (and eco-warrior) Clifford Jones, and this clearly struck a nerve with the Third Doctor. Was he, like, totes gel of the younger gent's relationship with Ms. Grant? His drive off into the sunset did seem to suggest some unseen involvement together.

River Song

Another woman who received her fair shares of good-byes with the Doctor, River's most touching moment came in "The Name of the Doctor" (2013). Thinking he couldn't see her, the Eleventh Doctor surprisingly revealed he could, in fact, see his "dead" wife. Visibly shocked, River soon composed herself for a big old smoochy with her hubby. Though this is, perhaps, not their last good-bye.

Rose Tyler

The feels! Poor Rose. She got more than one good-bye with her Time Lord, the Tenth Doctor, but let's look at her desperately affecting separation from her BFF in "Doomsday" (2006). The Time Lord did his best to give his friend a proper good-bye—burning up a sun just to break through the universes to bring her to Bad Wolf Bay. As a projection, the Gallifreyan and the human female spoke what they thought would be their final words together: "I love you," Rose emotionally pleaded, only to see him disappear into the ether.

Sarah Jane Smith

After spending so much time with the Doctor, Sarah Jane's departure from the TARDIS was sudden, fun, and slightly heartbreaking. Having dispatched evil Eldrad in 1976's "The Hand of Fear," the Fourth Doctor was recalled to Gallifrey, and informed his best friend that she would be unable to come. Initially thinking her buddy was having a jape, Sarah Jane realized the Time Lord was serious. "Don't forget me," she said, while he retorted, "Oh, Sarah—don't you forget me." The couple went on to share more farewells, even more teary and more heartbreaking.

Wilf Mott

Uh-oh, set the tear ducts to overload! The Tenth Doctor's buddy and the chap that kinda sorta killed him (but let's not dwell on that) had his fair share of fun with the Time Lord, but their parting was as touching as any companion, and, in fact, probably more so. After some visits to old friends in "The End of Time" (2010), the Doctor returned to visit Wilf at Donna's wedding, bonding one final time with his former companion's grandfather. The two men acknowledged the painful moment with a heartfelt and beautiful salute.

10 *Doctor Who* Stories You Might Not Know

Sure, you know all about the Doctor's normal television adventures, but what about those special scenes, sketches, and stories that passed you by? We've left out high-profile adventures such as 2007's "Time Crash" and Paul McGann's "The Night of the Doctor" (2013) along with all the "prequels" and DVD extra scenes (as they "technically" didn't air on television).

"A Fix with Sontarans" (1985)

This year saw the first of its kind with this specially written story starring Colin Baker and Janet Fielding as the Sixth Doctor and Tegan, respectively. Broadcast on BBC's children's show *Jim'll Fix It* (where kids were granted their wishes), it saw two Sontarans invade the TARDIS and the Doctor use a human boy to save the day.

"Dimensions in Time" (1993)

This two-parter from the 30th Anniversary year has never been repeated and never been released on any form of home video. There is a very good reason for that but let's focus on this story, which aired to help the fundraising activities for the UK non-profit organization Children in Need. This glorious mess saw numerous former Doctors and companions battle it out with former aliens and monsters and the cast of long-running UK soap *Eastenders*.

The Curse of Fatal Death (1999)

Now this one is actually quite good. This 1999 Comic Relief special was written by Steven Moffat, who eventually became *Doctor Who* showrunner, and starred Rowan Atkinson as the Doctor and Jonathan Pryce as the Master. After a Dalek attack, hilarity ensues as the Time Lord then regenerates into Richard E. Grant (who would go on to voice the "Ninth Doctor" in the 2003 web series *Scream of the Shalka*), Jim Broadbent, Hugh Grant, and then, finally, Joanna Lumley.

"Attack of the Graske" (2005)

This would be the first of many ancillary stories to accompany *Doctor Who* in its new Golden Age. Written by Gareth Roberts (2008's "The Unicorn and the Wasp"), it's technically a game, as it's an interactive episode that appeared on the BBC Red Button service just after "The

Christmas Invasion" aired on Christmas 2005. It's got David Tennant in it and you as the companion!

The Infinite Quest (2007)

This thirteen-episode animated epic featured the voices of David Tennant as the Tenth Doctor and Freema Agyeman as companion Martha Jones, and was broadcast as three-and-a-half minute installments in the spin-off show *Totally Doctor Who*, on BBC One in 2007. Anthony Head, best known in the world of *Who* as Finch from "School Reunion" (2006), provides the voice for the villain of the piece, space pirate Baltazar.

"Music of the Spheres" (2008–09)

And up pop the Graske again! The *Doctor Who Proms* in 2008 saw this wonderful slice of fun from Russell T. Davies with David Tennant. It actually premiered on the radio first, and then found its way on to television as part of the concert broadcast later that year. And there were more Proms to be had over the years, with Matt Smith filming scenes in 2010 and 2013.

Dreamland (2009)

Another animated adventure for the Tenth Doctor, and this time David Tennant is joined by actress Georgia Moffett, best known as Jenny in "The Doctor's Daughter" (in real life, she's also the daughter of Fifth Doctor Peter Davison and the real-life wife of the aforementioned Tenth Doctor, David Tennant). Its six parts (clocking in at forty-seven minutes) were first made available on the BBC's Red Button service and then broadcast as an omnibus edition featuring all the installments. Set in Roswell, New Mexico, in 1958, they show the Time Lord checking out Area 51 and all sorts of goings-on. It also features the voices of David Warner (2013's "Cold War") and Stuart Milligan (2011's "The Impossible Astronaut"/"Day of the Moon"). *Dreamland* was written by Phil Ford (2009's "The Waters of Mars"), who managed to connect it with his story "Prisoner of the Judoon" (2009) from *The Sarah Jane Adventures*.

"Death Is the Only Answer" (2011)

Written by the children of Oakley Junior School, this was the winning entry in a competition for children to write a short script for *Doctor Who*. Featuring Albert Einstein and an Ood, this lovely TARDIS-based story aired as part of *Doctor Who Confidential* on BBC Three (which followed "The Wedding of River Song," the BBC One premiere, in October 2011).

"Good as Gold" (2012)

More competition fun here, as this Olympic-themed short was penned by the Children of Ashdene School. This time, since *Doctor Who Confidential* had been cruelly canceled, it was run in conjunction with BBC children's show *Blue Peter* (which has a very long association with *Doctor Who*). Matt Smith and Karen Gillan starred alongside a Weeping Angel and a confused-looking athlete.

Pond Life (2012)

Finishing this collection is this rather beautiful and sad tale from writer Chris Chibnall (2012's "Dinosaurs on a Spaceship"), and it's another BBC Red Button adventure (and also online). Initially in five parts (though later collated for an omnibus version), *Pond Life* saw the break-up of Rory and Amy, and an Ood on the toilet. Chris also wrote the even more emotional short postscript that looked at Brian Williams' life after the departure of his son and daughter-in-law. It was only a webcast (with sketch drawings and narration from Arthur Darvill), so it doesn't get its own entry, sadly.

Where Have I Seen That Face Before?

Over the years, the Doctor has met many varied and different people, and sometimes he meets the same person (though, perhaps, not in that order). But on some occasions the Gallifreyan comes across people who look exactly like other people he's met elsewhere. On seeing *Torchwood*'s Gwen Cooper, after saving the universe from Davros and his reality bomb in "Journey's End" (2008), the Tenth Doctor commented on her similarity to Gwyneth, whom he and Rose had met in Cardiff in 1869 (during 2005's "The Unquiet Dead"), citing a "spatial genetic multiplicity." Well, whatever you call it, it's uncanny—and here are some familiar faces throughout the Whoniverse.

Captain Hardaker

While he did partake in Max Capricorn's sabotage of the *Titanic* (the spaceship, not the doomed Earth-based sealiner) in "Voyage of the Damned" (2007), Captain Hardaker did have extenuating circumstances (he did it for the good of his family). An honorable chap to be sure, if slightly misguided, he did share a passing resemblance with some humans involved in adventures with the Doctor, and equally short-lived. Both Edward Masters and the Administrator of Solos could be younger versions of Hardaker. The former faced a grisly death after being infected by a Silurian virus in "Doctor Who and the Silurians" (1970), while the latter was assassinated by a Solonian (just before he was to grant independence to Solos from the Earth Empire in the thirtieth century) in "The Mutants" (1972). All were played by UK television legend Geoffrey Palmer.

Mr. Copper

Another entry here from the 2007 Christmas special, "Voyage of the Damned," which featured a helpful fellow who looked incredibly similar to another chap the Time Lord met some regenerations previous in "Revelation of the Daleks" (1985). Jobel, a slightly more ginger and moustachier version of Copper, wanted to dispose of Davros (while going under the moniker the Great Healer at the Tranquil Repose on Necros), but his treachery, not to mention lechery, were undone by his loyal assistant, Tasambeker, who killed him. Both were portayed by Clive Swift.

Val

The Eleventh Doctor and Craig Owens met Val while investigating odd goings-on at the Sanderson & Grainger department store in Colchester, England, in "Closing Time" (2011). A friendly type, Val assisted with their detective work (which led to the uncovering of a Cybermen plot) and even thought that the two men were more than just friends. But could the lovely shop assistant be related, in some way, to Captain Wrack, an Eternal who worked alongside the Black Guardian in the 1983 Peter Davison four-parter "Enlightenment"? Could be. And her voice? I'm sure she was singing when the First Doctor visited Tombstone, Arizona, in 1881 during "The Gunfighters" (1966). Actress Lynda Baron was the lady behind all of these characters.

Florence Finnegan

The 2007 opener, "Smith and Jones," introduced us to this Plasmavore, but the would-be killer of the Tenth Doctor was not dissimilar to human female Nurse Crane encountered in "The Curse of Fenric" (1989). The Seventh Doctor and Ace came into contact with her during World War II on Earth in an attack by Fenric and its Haemovores—she died at the hands of the monsters. English actress Anne Reid played both these roles.

Colonel Hugh Curbishley

The Colonel met the Tenth Doctor and Donna Noble in a sleepy English village in the 2008 romp "The Unicorn and the Wasp." He was wheelchair-bound, though this was a ruse to ensure his beautiful wife didn't leave him for another man (tsk tsk). An elderly man, for sure, but if you picture him thirty/forty years younger, then you have the very image of Henry Gordon Jago, the rambunctious theater owner who assisted the Fourth Doctor and Leela in their fight against Magnus Greel in "The Talons of Weng Chiang" (1977). And there's also Keith Gold, director of the Inferno Project on Earth during the 1970s, which saw the Third Doctor encounter a parallel Earth (where Keith was already dead) in "Inferno" (1970). All three were played by the chameleon-like Christopher Benjamin.

Count Carlos Scarlioni

For many, "City of Death" (1979) is one of *the* greatest Doctor Who stories *ever*. Although alien in form (and a pretty disgusting one at that), Scaroth took the human persona of Scarlioni, who, rather

strangely, could have been the brother of Richard the Lionheart (with a little beard) from "The Crusade" (1965). The King helped out the First Doctor during the 1190 Crusades in retrieving the kidnapped Barbara, and he later knighted school teacher Chesterton as Sir Ian of Jaffa. Julian Glover was the man responsible for these creations, and you'll find him elsewhere in another list, too!

Chantho

The lovely (though slightly tragic) alien Chantho, who met the Tenth Doctor, Martha Jones, and Captain Jack in "Utopia" (2007), may not resemble a human, but if you look really closely, you might see some kind of similarity with the fortune-teller Donna Noble met on the planet Shan Shen while traveling with the Tenth Doctor, from "Turn Left" the following year. At first she seemed like a pleasant type, but she soon created a new universe, changing the Chiswick temp's time line (briefly), as the fortune-teller was revealed to be a part of the Trickster's Brigade! The equally exotically named Chipo Chung brought both of these characters to life on-screen.

Francine Jones

You have to look really, really hard to spot the likeness here. Martha's mother, Francine, whom we first met in the 2007 opener, "Smith and Jones," was a bit of a cow toward the man who dragged her daughter away through space and time, and found herself inadvertently aiding the Master (who also enslaved Mrs. Jones for one year aboard the *Valiant*). Her alter ego, Sister Jatt, was just as catty when the Tenth Doctor bumped into the Catnun in New New York in "New Earth" (2006). She died when touched by one of the many "patients" that the Sisters of Plentitude "cared" for. Cat and human were played by Adjoa Andoh.

Laurence Scarman

Lovely Laurence befriended the Fourth Doctor and Sarah Jane Smith after his own brother was taken by Sutekh in the early twentieth century on Earth. A polite and friendly soul, Scarman helped the Time Lord defeat the nasty deity in "Pyramids of Mars" (1975). Oddly, the Doctor never commented on the numerous men who could have been Scarman's doppelganger. Before this meeting, the First Doctor met Rhos on board the Ark, in "The Ark" (1966), while the Third Doctor encountered Dr. Roland Summers at Stangmoor Prison (where the Keller Machine was being used to alter people's minds) in "The Mind of Evil" (1971), and then the Fourth Doctor himself met Lowe in "The Invisible Enemy" (1977), and then his fifth and sixth incarnations met Mergrave in the Master's illusory world in "Castrovalva" (1982), and finally a London Headmaster in 1988's "Remembrance of the Daleks"—all men the very image of Scarman! *Doctor Who* legend Michael Sheard was the talent behind so many great characters—and another actor whom you can find elsewhere in these lists.

Professor Hobbes

This professor met the Tenth Doctor while they were both on a bus cruise on their way to a sapphire waterfall in the 2008 episode "Midnight." The doomed journey saw the men as friends, at first, but Hobbes turned against the Time Lord, along with the rest of the passengers of the trip. But, take a wander forward in time (yet back for the Doctor) and we note that Peladon (from 1972's "The Curse of Peladon") is the spitting image of Hobbes. Definitely a nice chap, though, even asking Jo Grant to marry him (sadly, for him, she declined his offer). A keen eye, and a good memory, will observe that Private Moor in "The War Games" (1969) and a guard in "The Enemy of the World" (1967) all share a younger semblance of the man. In fact, Patrick Troughton's son, David Troughton, with whom he shared two adventures on-screen, performed these roles.

Of Course, We Didn't Forget...

- **Amy Pond** bore a striking resemblance to a soothsayer during the Tenth's Doctor's visit to Pompeii (Karen Gillan in 2008's "The Fires of Pompeii")

- **Harry Sullivan** could have had a twin in ship officer John Andrews (whom the Third Doctor met on the SS *Bernice* in 1973's "Carnival of Monsters"), both played by Ian Marter

- **First Doctor companion Steven** had an uncanny other in "American" tourist Morton Dill, whom the Doctor met shortly before Steven joined the TARDIS in 1965's "The Chase" (thanks to Peter Purves)

- Many years after **Barbara Wright** left her time-traveling days behind, the Fourth Doctor encountered her look-alike, priestess Lexa, on Tigella in 1979's "The Creature from the Pit" (as portrayed by Jacqueline Hill

- Martha Jones' cousin, **Adeola Oshodi** (who worked for Torchwood in "Army of Ghosts" and died at the hands of the Tenth Doctor, kind of), was played by the lovely Freema Agyeman

- The **Brigadier** surely had a brother in Space Security Agent Bret Vyon (who helped the First Doctor battle the Daleks), the legendary Nicholas Courtney

- **Sixth Doctor Colin Baker** even had a double in Maxil in "Arc of Infinity" (1983)

- And we're sure we've seen the **Twelfth Doctor** somewhere before…

That Sounds Nice, Let's Go There!

The Doctor is often talking about places we've never seen, some more glamorous-sounding than others. Below you'll find some of the more exotic locales mentioned but never seen by various characters since 2005.

Asgard

2008's "Silence in the Library" revealed that the Doctor and River Song had a picnic there at some point in their relationship. Maybe we'll see Peter Capaldi and Alex Kingston there one day...

Barcelona

Shortly before he became David Tennant, Christopher Eccleston told Billie Piper all about the planet Barcelona in "The Parting of the Ways" (2005): "Fantastic place. They've got dogs with no noses." The Tenth Doctor also name-checked it in "The Fires of Pompeii" (2008).

Catrigan Nova

In "The Last of the Time Lords" (2007), the Master told his masseuse, Tanya, he would take her there.

Darillium

River Song, in 2008's "Forest of the Dead," reminisced before she died about her trip to see the Singing Towers on the planet: "What a night that was. The Towers sang, and you cried."

Felspoon

According to Donna Noble, after she'd become the Doctor/Donna in "Journey's End" (2008), this planet has "mountains that sway in the breeze."

Kataa Flo Ko

When he thought that Donna Noble was leaving him for good, the Tenth Doctor revealed he wanted to take her to see the diamond coral reefs on this planet. Also mentioned by the Time Lord as possible destinations in "The Sontaran Stratagem" (2008) are Fifteenth Broken Moon of the Medusa Cascade and the Lightning Skies of Cotter Palluni's World.

Meta Sigma Folio

In a bid to keep Martha Jones as a TARDIS traveler in "The Last of the Time Lords" (2007), the Tenth Doctor tempted her with a trip to see a "burst of starfire right now over the coast of Meta Sigma Folio," where she would also note the "sky is like oil on water."

Phosphorous Carousel of the Great Magellan Gestadt

The Tenth Doctor took a trip there before his regeneration, as mentioned to Ood Sigma in "The End of Time Part One" (2009).

Woman Wept

Rose told Mickey all about this planet in "Boom Town" (2005). So called as there was a continent that looked like a lamenting woman from above, Woman Wept was cold and featured huge beaches that were met by ice waves, hundreds of feet high. It was also taken by Davros in "The Stolen Earth" (2008).

Welsh Rare Bit

Very rare, indeed. Despite Cardiff, the capital of Wales, being the very home of *Doctor Who*, the show has actually rarely set any stories in the country. In fact, there was only one before the show came back in 2005. Check out the Welsh connections below.

"The Green Death" (1973)

Shockingly, the Doctor didn't visit Wales for the best part of a decade in his TV show. It was not until the final story for companion Jo Grant that the Time Lord visited in this seventies eco-tale with giant maggots in Llanfairfach. It also proved to be the final story for Jo Grant, who left the Doctor to marry Nobel Prize winner Professor Clifford Jones.

"The Unquiet Dead" (2005)

The Ninth Doctor had initially intended to take his new BFF, Rose, to Christmas Eve in Naples in 1860; however, things went slightly awry as the intrepid twosome actually ended up in Cardiff, 1869—much to his companion's annoyance. Luckily for them, Charles Dickens was in town with a bunch of ghosts to keep them entertained.

"Boom Town" (2005)

Team TARDIS, featuring Nine, Rose, and Captain Jack, popped over to Cardiff to refuel the Doctor's ship at the Rift. Sensing a holiday was in order, Mickey took a trip over from London to spend a romantic night with his girlfriend. Cardiff Bay never looked lovelier, until it was ripped apart in an evil plan by Margaret Slitheen.

"Utopia"/"The Last of the Time Lords" (2007)

More modern-day Cardiff fun here as the Tenth Doctor made a pit stop at the Rift, and an eager Captain Jack Harkness jumped on board, literally, the TARDIS. After an adventure far in the future, and a missing year, the last of the Time Lords and companion Martha Jones returned Jack to Torchwood after an emotional farewell in front of the Millennium Centre.

"The Stolen Earth"/"Journey's End" (2008)

The Torchwood base came under attack by those pesky Daleks in the Series 4 finale. Thankfully, for Gwen and Ianto (the Torchwood staff left there), a time lock prevented Skaro's finest from penetrating and exterminating.

"The Hungry Earth"/"Cold Blood" (2010)

The Eleventh Doctor, Amy, and Rory were on their way to Rio, Brazil, when the TARDIS took a detour and landed them in Cwmtaff, Wales, in 2020. Here the gang bumped into some Silurians who weren't too happy at the drilling going on. Oddly, even though the *homo reptilia* were based in Wales, there wasn't a Welsh accent to be heard underground.

"Death of the Doctor" (2010)

And just for good measure, here's a story from the brilliant spin-off series *The Sarah Jane Adventures*. It starred Matt Smith as the Eleventh Doctor, which is why we can include it here. This two-parter (which also starred Katy Manning as Jo Jones, née Grant) saw Sarah Jane and her mates visit a UNIT base in Mount Snowden.

Whose Booze?

Though often showing disdain for alcohol, the Doctor does sometimes imbibe in the devil's juice. But, remember, please drink responsibly.

The First Doctor

If you're looking for a boozefest, then check out "The Smugglers" (1966). During the story, companion Ben Jackson quaffed some beer, and you'll see brandy used as a motivator for sailors on the *Black Albatross*, while the Doctor himself enjoyed a "very fine old Madeira." The naughty Time Lord also took some mead in "The Time Meddler" (1965) and even treated the TARDIS crew to some champagne on Christmas Day in "The Daleks' Master Plan" (1965). In "The Romans" (1965) companion Vicki Pallister took on Nero by poisoning a goblet of wine.

The Second Doctor

He was also a wine fan, drinking some in "The Evil of the Daleks" (1967), though he wouldn't be seen to enjoy much else during his time.

The Third Doctor

A slightly keener aficionado was Jon Pertwee's suave incarnation. "Colony in Space" (1971), "The Sea Devils" (1972), and "The Time Warrior" (1974) would all see him have a cheeky swifter, while "Day of the Daleks" (1972) saw the Gallifreyan claim, "That's a most good-humoured wine. A touch sardonic, perhaps, but not cynical. A most civilized wine, one after my own heart." Elsewhere in his time, booze was taken in "Carnival of Monsters" (1973), while the Brigadier said, "I'd rather have a pint," in "The Dæmons" (1971).

The Fourth Doctor

The 1979 classic "City of Death" (1979) found Tom Baker and Lalla Ward in Paris, and the "table wine" of a year, did see some liquor on show from the Countess. In his second story, "The Ark in Space" (1975), the Fourth Doctor revealed he kept brandy as he tried to help an unconscious Sarah Jane Smith. Baker's last season in the TARDIS saw a veritable celebration of wine in 1980's "State of Decay" and in the subsequent episodes "Warriors' Gate" (which saw the Time Lord sup) and "The Keeper of Traken."

The Fifth through Eighth Doctors

The decadence of the eighties was countered by *Doctor Who*'s sobriety during the decade. In "The Visitation" (1982), traveling actor Richard Mace was a huge wine fan, looking for some that tasted like "nectar" in a cellar with Adric. In the same story a "posset" was unveiled, though it would not reach its intended due to the beam of a Terileptil android. Soon after, in "Black Orchid" (1982), Tegan Jovanka partook in a screwdriver, while Adric could only look on in envy.

Wine reared its head again in Colin Baker's story "The Two Doctors" (1985), where twelve bottles of wine were required, and in the 1996 TV Movie, plenty of champagne was being enjoyed at the year 2000 party in San Francisco.

The Ninth Doctor

In his brief time, Christopher Eccleston clocked up a few alcohol moments. In "Rose" (2005), he used a bottle of champagne to attack Auton Mickey Smith, and he would go on to threaten the Slitheen with brandy a few episodes later in "World War Three" (and then have a sip later, which he didn't seem to enjoy). Sticking with the inhabitants of Raxacoricofallapatorius, Nine dined with Margaret (or Blon Fel-Fotch Passameer-Day Slitheen) with some wine (in which she tried to poison him). And, of course, the ever-gregarious Captain Jack Harkness took in a vermouth-heavy martini in "The Doctor Dances" (also 2005).

The Tenth Doctor

Champagne was the drink of choice in the David Tennant era, featuring in 2006's "New Earth" (where it was refused by the Doctor) and "Rise of the Cybermen" (where is was served at Pete Tyler's party), as well as 2007's "Voyage of the Damned" (where the Time Lord used a bottle to spray some rather unpleasant passengers). More famously, the Tenth Doctor thought he invented the banana daiquiri in 2006's "The Girl in the Fireplace" (seemingly under the influence), while companion Donna Noble consumed a sidecar in 2008's "The Unicorn and the Wasp" (an episode which also saw her mention a Harvey Wallbanger).

The Eleventh Doctor

Matt Smith's youthful take on the Doctor displayed a disdain for drink. In both "The Lodger" (2010) and "The Impossible Astronaut" (2011), he spit out wine, though his missus was quite fond of booze, drinking champagne "disgracefully" in "The Name of the Doctor" (2013) and sharing some wine with Dorium Maldovar in 2010's "The Pandorica Opens" (though she did just spike his drink with micro-explosives). Companion Clara described whiskey as the "eleventh most disgusting thing ever invented" in "Hide" (2013), and it was revealed in "The Wedding of River Song" (2011) that the Brigadier asked for an extra brandy to be poured should his old friend ever return.

9 Fantastic Things about the Ninth Doctor

The year 2005 was the year of *Doctor Who* and Christopher Eccleston. But what makes his incarnation of the Time Lord just so darn good? Here's why.

9. "Fantastic!"

His catchphrase is said by the Ninth Doctor in all but one of his stories ("The Long Game," in case you're wondering.)

8. Jackie Tyler

In their very first meeting, the Gallifreyan rebukes the bedroom advances of Rose's mother ("Rose"). He paid for it, however, in "Aliens of London," when he got slapped for taking Jackie's daughter away for a year.

7. "I can feel it. The turn of the Earth…"

"The ground beneath our feet is spinning at a thousand miles an hour, and the entire planet is hurtling round the sun at sixty-seven thousand miles an hour, and I can feel it. We're falling through space, you and me, clinging to the skin of this tiny little world, and if we let go. That's who I am." Amazingly, this scene was added to "Rose" very late, as it ran short of its forty-five-minute time slot.

6. Flirty

Jabe, Margaret Slitheen, Lynda, and even Captain Jack Harkness—no one was safe from the roving eye of Nine.

5. The Doctor meets Dickens

Stuck in a cab with his hero in "The Unquiet Dead," the Doctor gets to gush about the author's work. It's a lovely moment, mirroring the worship that exists, in real life, around *Doctor Who*. Though a fan, he's never scared to be slightly critical—regarding the "American bit" in *Martin Chuzzlewit*, he states, "Was that just padding or what? I mean, it's rubbish, that bit!"

4. Leather Jacket

The Ninth Doctor's fashion was quite unlike that of any of his predecessors. No ties or scarves or waistcoats or frilly shirts, Nine was a tough guy—though he did occasionally change his jumper, which he was very self-conscious about ("The Unquiet Dead").

3. Stand-Up Comedian

In the midst of war, the Gallifreyan inadvertently began his short-lived career as a stand-up comedian in "The Empty Child."

2. He Regenerated Standing Up!

Another first for *Doctor Who*. In the olden times—you know, pre-Internet—Time Lords did it lying down. But in this new age, *nobody* does it on the floor—that's so "classic." These days, the Doctor does it standing up, and Eccleston was the first to regenerate on his feet ("The Parting of the Ways").

1. It's Christopher Eccleston!

Already a highly respected actor of television and theater, Eccleston brought a real sense of drama to the role of the Doctor. His face-offs with the villains were all the more believable because of his skills as an actor. He hasn't returned to *Doctor Who* yet, but hopefully some day…

10 Brilliant Things about the Tenth Doctor

Hot on the heels of the show's revival in 2005 came another new Doctor—in the shape of David Tennant. He stayed until the first day of the next decade and won millions of fans along the way. Here's why.

10. There's Two of Them!

Yup, in "Journey's End" (2008), every fangirl's (and some fanboy's) dream came true—Double Tennant. Due to his hand-in-a-jar and some intervention from Donna Noble, the world of *Doctor Who* was rocked with two versions of the Doctor running around the universe. Captain Jack was *very* pleased.

9. Companions

He had great taste in friends: Rose—she broke through universes just to find him; Martha—she saved the world, by herself; and Donna—she became part Time Lord and helped defeat Davros!

8. Words

The Tenth Doctor loved words, absolutely adored them. Just listen to the way he says "conglomeration" in "Utopia" (2007), and "Strictly speaking, it's the fifteenth New York since the original, so that makes it New-New-New-New-New-New-New-New-New-New-New-New-New-New-New New York" in "New Earth" (2006), or invents the classic "timey-wimey wibbly-wobbly" in "Blink" (2007).

7. Glasses

Or "Brainy Specs," as he refers to them in "Time Crash" (2007). Tennant heralded geek chic with these eye accessories. No longer was it uncool to wear glasses. Of course, he only wears them because he thinks they make him look clever.

6. He Defeated the DEVIL!

Well, with a little help from Rose he did anyway (2006's "The Satan Pit").

5. He Forgave the Master

Almost as soon as his fellow Time Lord, the Master, returned and they were saying goodbye. "I forgive you," soothes Ten as his foe curls into a ball. Now, given what the rather evil renegade had done (decimated the Earth and so forth), that was quite a lot. Sadly, the bad boy died in the Doctor's arms, causing a number of tears from the Gallifreyan. Speaking of which…

4. Emotions

Blimey, this regeneration had plenty of them! Just a few episodes in on his run and he fell in love with Madame de Pompadour in "The Girl in the Fireplace" (2006) before burning up a sun just to say good-bye to Rose in "Doomsday" in the same year. Ten was very much a man in touch with his heart.

3. Became Human to Help His Enemies

In "Human Nature" (2007), the Doctor transformed himself using the Chameleon Arch to avoid being hunted down by the Family of Blood, who could sniff out a Time Lord across the galaxy. But it's not until his enemy is defeated that we discover exactly why he set out to hide and avoid being found by the Family. The son, in the form of schoolboy Baines, said, "He was being kind. We wanted to live forever, so the Doctor made sure that we did." The Doctor didn't want to have dish out justice and so went through the distressing process of humanisizing himself in order to save them.

2. He Didn't Want to Go

And we didn't want him to go, either! The world cried as his TARDIS exploded around him and he sadly stated, "I don't wanna go," as the regeneration process took hold in "The End of Time" (2010). Sniff, still hurts.

1. It's David Tennant!

Almost as soon as David appeared as the Tenth Doctor, the world fell in love with his roguish charm, twinkly eyes, and engaging smile. Apart from the fact that he was a fan (and became an actor just to become the Doctor), David also made scores of appearances on television promoting the show, sharing his enthusiasm and spreading the love.

11 Lovely Things about the Eleventh Doctor

Stealing our collective hearts while bellowing "Geronimo!" and donning a Fez, Matt Smith, for many, will always be *the* Doctor. And here are eleven reasons why.

11. Wig!

You may not know this, but in "The Time of the Doctor" (2013), Matt wore a wig as he'd shaved his head for a part in a film, 2014's *Lost River*. (Fact fans will note that he also wore a wig in 2011's "Day of the Moon.")

10. He Wanted to Be a Redhead

In the dramatic closing moments of "The End of Time" (2010), the Eleventh Doctor lamented he was "still not ginger" after his regeneration. Maybe all that time with Donna Noble rubbed off on him. Regardless, his first companion, Amy Pond, provided some much-needed hair color in the TARDIS.

9. Dancing Skills

"I only came for the dancing!" he beams in "The Big Bang" (2010), and just check out those moves. Despite being dubbed "embarrassing" by Amy, the Time Lord rocked on with what is lovingly referred to as the "Drunk Giraffe" (copyright Steven Moffat).

8. He Traveled with a Married Couple

Even before they were the Ponds, Amy and Rory were the Doctor's TARDIS buddies. After their marriage, they shared a bunk bed, though he did rectify that situation soon after the couple's nuptials.

7. He Rebooted the Universe

Yeah, just that! (2010's "The Big Bang")

6. Bow Tie and Tweed

The Eleventh Doctor single-handedly brought the bow tie back into the fashion consciousness. Not only that, sales of tweed jackets skyrocketed soon after its debut in "The Eleventh Hour" (2010).

5. Speaks Baby

As demonstrated in his conversations with Melody Pond in "A Good Man Goes to War" (2011) and Craig Owens' son, Stormageddon, in "Closing Time" (2011).

4. Married River Song

Well, we think they got married. The Doctor was, in fact, inside the Teselecta which married River Song (in order to right time). That counts, right? Either way, they liked a good old snog every now and then.

3. Took Rory's Dad on Vacation

At the end of "Dinosaurs on a Spaceship" (2012), the Doctor treated Brian Pond to trips to New York, Rio de Janeiro, Pisa, Taj Mahal, Machu Picchu, and even Siluria. What a nice guy!

2. Got Two Totally Different Title Sequences

The last actor to benefit from being gifted two vastly different title sequences for *Doctor Who* was Tom Baker. Matt Smith also received his face in them, a feat unseen since 1989 with the Sylvester McCoy era.

1. It's Matt Smith!

Pretty much an unknown when he took on the role (though winning praise for his part in the wonderful BBC Two show *Party Animals*), Matt quickly won over everyone who said he was too young to play the part, and became *the* Doctor for millions across the world.

12 Things We Love about the Twelfth Doctor

With one series under his belt now (and having already appeared in fifteen episodes by the end of 2014), *Doctor Who* fans are firmly in love with the Twelfth Doctor. But why? Here are some reasons.

12. CapaldEyes!

His shocking cameo in "The Day of the Doctor" (2013) was made all the more shocking by his magnificent eyebrows! They would be constantly referred to in his first year in charge.

11. Dino Love

"Deep Breath" (2014) displayed that he wasn't averse to dinosaur romance when one turned up in the Thames (after spitting out the TARDIS).

10. Mean Streak

Not half! In his first outing, we're pretty sure he pushed that poor Half-Faced Man onto Big Ben's spire, and then the following week, he lets a poor rebel get blasted by a Dalek's antibodies.

9. Doesn't Understand What a Fake ID Is For

In "The Caretaker" (2014), he assumed that Coal Hill School pupil (and first female U.S. President) Courtney Woods used his physic paper as a fake ID to get into museums, and not to buy booze with. Aw, silly old Doctor.

8. Is Scared of the Dark

Aw, poor Twelve! "Listen" (2014) showed us the origins of his fear on Gallifrey in the space barn. Bored one day, the Twelfth Doctor sought out the reasons why…

7. Has an Invisible Watch

You know, this could have come in handy for the Doctor and his many chums numerous times over the years. Better than a perception filter, this thing actually makes you invisible. However, don't think about wearing one and surprising the Doctor, as he can feel a light shield aura when it's right next to him.

6. Doesn't Like PE teachers

Who does? In "The Caretaker" (2014), we saw the Twelfth Doctor firmly expound his views on them, mistaking Danny Pink for one.

5. Uses the Phrase, "Big Man!"

Very common in Scotland, Peter Capaldi's home country, this affectionate term has been hijacked by the Twelfth Doctor a few times already. In "Deep Breath" (2014), he refers to the Thames T-Rex as "Big Man" (and then corrects himself with "Big Woman!"), while he calls the Teller the very same thing in "Time Heist" (2014). The Doctor mixes it up slightly in "Into the Dalek" (2014) where he uses "Big Fella" to describe the rebel spacecraft, the Aristotle.

4. Likes to Save Species

Both "Time Heist" and "Kill The Moon" (2014) displayed the Doctor's love for rare species. And, coincidentally, neither race of creatures was named.

3. Fights with a Spoon!

Robin Hood may well have had a sword to fight off enemies, but everyone's favorite Gallifreyan only needed a simple kitchen utensil, the spoon! One of the Time Lord's predecessor's, the Seventh Doctor, also liked the spoons—he used to play them. Must be a Scottish thing…

2. Uses a Yo-Yo!

In the brilliant episode "Kill the Moon" (2014), the Doctor utilized a yo-yo in order to measure the gravity of the situation on board the space shuttle. He then tried to save Courtney Woods with it and used to it to discover the moon had amniotic fluid under the surface. The Fourth Doctor was also very keen on yo-yos, using one on many occasions.

1. It's Peter Capaldi!

The Scottish actor had made a name for himself in the UK in the sitcom *The Thick of It*, where he played a slightly grumpy and sweary Scotsman (where do they get their ideas from?). Capaldi had already starred in 2008's "The Fires of Pompeii" and in *Torchwood: Children of Earth* the following year, so he was known to Who fans. And, like David Tennant, he is a pure 100 percent *Doctor Who* FAN!

Top 11 "Other" Doctors

Aside from the familiar names of First Doctor William Hartnell through to Twelfth Doctor Peter Capaldi, there have been other actors who have played the Time Lord on television and film. Here are some you might have missed.

The Morbius Doctors

When the Fourth Doctor faced-off against Morbius, another renegade Time Lord, in the 1976 story "The Brain of Morbius," a mental battle between the two took place, which seemed to show some past regenerations of the Doctor before William Hartnell. Fact fans may love that the previous Doctors were all involved in the *Doctor Who* production team, including luminaries such as directors Graeme Harper and Douglas Camfield, and writers Philip Hinchcliffe, Robert Banks Stewart, and Robert Holmes, among others.

The Fatal Death Doctor(s)

Okay, this is a slight cheat, but if you want to know why he's on the list, we'll explain later. Steven Moffat penned a delightful *Doctor Who* mini-story for Comic Relief back in 1999, a ball of timey-wimey goodness with the usual fun Moffery. Starring Rowan Atkinson (best known for Mr. Bean) as the Doctor, "The Curse of Fatal Death" pitted the Time Lord and his assistant, played by Julia Swahala (who had previously turned down a role as companion in *Who*), against the Master (played by Jonathan Pryce) and the Daleks. Of course, Atkinson would himself regenerate in the story into numerous familiar faces.

Robot Dr. Who

The classic 1966 six-part Dalek story "The Chase" has a lot of memorable, not to mention fun, moments (Dracula and his buddies and Empire State Building tomfoolery, for example), but perhaps the most interesting, and I'm speaking euphemistically here, is the appearance of Dalek creation the Robot Dr. Who (as was titled in the credits, don't get angry!). Despite being played by "double" (to use the word loosely) Edmund Warwick, the mechanical version of the Time Lord managed to fool his chums (perhaps because his voice was dubbed by William Hartnell), leaving trusty companion Ian Chesterton to nearly kill the *real* Doctor in a fight. Please note: Other robot/android/doppleganger Doctors can also be seen in "The Android Invasion" (1975), "Meglos" (1980), "Arc of Infinity" (1983), et al.

Mawdryn

This wily fellow popped up in the Fifth Doctor 1983 four-parter "Mawdryn Undead." With his skull opened, revealing a pinky bulbous and wiry brain, he stumbled aboard the TARDIS and convinced the Fifth Doctor's fellow travelers, Nysaa and Tegan, that he was, in fact, the Doctor, merely regenerated. Mawdryn was traveling with fellow scientists who were seeking the secret of Time Lord regeneration, but had discovered, however, a life of the undead being unable to die. So, really, not the Doctor—but a Doctor wannabe.

The Watcher

"He was the Doctor all the time!" proclaimed smarty-pants companion Nysaa as this faded, ghost-like creeper merged with Tom Baker's Fourth Doctor and transformed the curly-headed, wide-teethed one into the much more pleasant and affable Fifth Doctor, as played by Peter Davison. The Watcher was an eerie figure that cast a huge shadow over the four-part swan song for Baker, "Logopolis" (1981), and was an immense addition to the show's oeuvre, suggesting that the Doctor can help his past self when it comes to regeneration.

The Shalka Doctor

Shortly after the return of Doctor Who was announced in 2003 came this animated web series that had ditched Paul McGann as the Doctor and plowed on with a Ninth Doctor, his Withnail & I co-star, Richard E. Grant. Celebrating the show's 40th Anniversary, Scream of the Shalka (2003) was made available on the official website (and it's still there!) and had quite the cast, also featuring Derek Jacobi (as the Master, no less, a few years before his proper small-screen debut as the renegade Time Lord), Sophie Okonedo (who would also pop on TV as Liz Ten), and a little guy known as David Tennant. Fact fans will note that Grant already played "the Doctor" in "The Curse of Fatal Death" (1999).

(Now, due to the events of "The Name of the Doctor," is it possible to retro-fit the Great Intelligence as an incarnation of everyone's favorite Gallifreyan, albeit briefly?)

The Dalek Movies Dr.

Good old Peter Cushing starred as Dr. Who (yup, you read correctly) in the two fantastic Dalek movies from the mid-sixties, Dr. Who and the Daleks and Daleks' Invasion Earth 2150 AD. But rather than being an alien, a wanderer in space and time, Cushing's role was that of an Earth-based scientist who built his own time-travel machine, TARDIS (they dropped the definite article, fact fans). He plays it for laughs, largely, in the debut, but the Hammer actor is perfect in the brilliant sequel, putting in a performance that outshines a number that followed after him on television.

The Doctor/Donna

Or the Meta-Crisis Doctor, as some might say. This is what happens when your hand gets lopped off by a Sycorax on Christmas Day: said hand is kept in a reciprocal by a mysterious omni-sexual time agent and then returned to your TARDIS where it sits for a few adventures until it breaks open and bonds with a temp from Chiswick—the feisty human female Donna Noble. And out of that fiery start came the genocidal maniac who wasn't quite as compassionate as his original Tenth Doctor, but he *could* share his feelings with Rose Tyler, so we forgave him. Aw, the feels.

"The Next Doctor" Doctor

Much was made of the 2008 Christmas special and its "Next Doctor" David Morrissey, so much so that the actor himself played along with the thought that he might, in fact, be the new *Doctor Who*. Jackson Lake, as it turned out, had his mind fused with an Infostamp, containing information on the Doctor and his lives, in an encounter with the Cybermen in nineteenth-century London. Morrissey was a fan's dream, so perfect for the role (complete with archetypal, old-skool *Doctor Who* costume)—made so alive in his first doppleganger-esque meeting with David Tennant's Tenth Doctor as they brandished their "sonics" in the opening pre-titles sequence. One can still hope that the actor could make a return…

The Dream Lord

To paraphrase Dr. Belloq from *Raiders of the Lost Ark*, the Dream Lord is a shadowy reflection of the Doctor. Golden Globe–nominated actor Toby Jones lit up the screen as the Trickster messing with the minds of the Eleventh Doctor, Amy, and Rory in the cracking 2010 episode "Amy's Choice," from *Men Behaving Badly* writer Simon Nye. As a scrunched-up, more grotesque (but still bow tie–wearing) version of the Time Lord, the Dream Lord reveled in revealing the uncomfortable truth. Bizarrely, the little devil's plan seemed to be that he wanted to kill the Doctor which, we would assume, would have meant his own demise. Excitingly, the end of the episode displayed that the Dream Lord was not defeated, and perhaps lying dormant until the next time some psychic pollen arrives in the TARDIS.

The Valeyard

Talking of shadowy reflections, this guy was a huge figure during "The Trial of a Time Lord" (if you can sit through its sprawling fourteen-episode epicness). The Valeyard was "an amalgamation of the darker side

of the Doctor's nature" sitting somewhere between his twelfth and final regeneration (according to the Doctor's BFF, the Master). He took delight in goading and prodding himself during the tiresome trial, but his plan to take the Doctor's remaining regenerations (and also to destroy the Time Lords) failed, though he would survive to fight another day (hopefully). Bat-eared viewers will have noted that the Great Intelligence name-checked the Valeyard when he had a showdown with the Doctor on Trenzalore.

15 Things You Never Knew the Sonic Did

Okay, you know the sonic screwdriver doesn't do wood, but here are fifteen uses of the sonic that may have passed you by!

15. **Works as an *actual* screwdriver!**
   "The War Games" (1969)
   "The Curse of Peladon" (1972)
   "The Ark in Space" (1975)
   "Castrovalva" (1982)
   "The Doctor's Daughter" (2008)

14. **Fixes barbed wire.**
   "The Doctor Dances" (2005)

13. **Cracks safes.**
   "The Sun Makers" (1977)

12. **Cash machine money-grabber.**
   "The Long Game" (2005)
   "The Runaway Bride" (2006)

11. **Enables phones to work through time and space.**
   "42" (2007)
   "The Doctor's Daughter" (2008)
   "Planet of the Dead" (2009)

10. **Giant Maggot–distractor.**
   "The Green Death" (1973)

9. **Candle/torch/Bunsen burner–lighter.**
   "The Girl in the Fireplace" (2006)
   "The Pandorica Opens" (2010)
   "Evolution of the Daleks" (2007)

8. **Toy activator.**
   "Night Terrors" (2011)

7. **Champagne bottle–uncorker.**
   "Voyage of the Damned" (2007)

6. **Space Whale vomit-inducer!**
   "The Beast Below" (2010)

5. **Land mine–detonator.**
   "The Sea Devils" (1972)

4. **"Trying to set up a resonation pattern in the concrete"**
   —the Ninth Doctor.
   "The Doctor Dances" (2005)

3. **Transforms glasses into sunglasses.**
   "Planet of the Dead" (2009)

2. **Lightbulb-exploder!**
   "Amy's Choice" (2010)

1. **Microphone.**
   "A Christmas Carol" (2010)
   "The God Complex" (2011)

Aliases of the Doctor

As a very special Time Lord, the Doctor just can't go out giving his actual name to everyone he meets (he does encounter rather a lot of people on his travels), so it's important that he has a pseudonym ready for the occasion. As you will see elsewhere, the Gallifreyan often opts for John Smith, but here you'll find all the other aliases he has used (or used by his companions on his behalf).

Theta Sigma
"The Armageddon Factor" (1979), "The Happiness Patrol" (1988), and in River Song's message from the dawn of time in "The Pandorica Opens" (2010).

?
"The Invasion of Time" (1978) and "Remembrance of the Daleks" (1988)—both signed on documents.

Sir Doctor of TARDIS
"Tooth and Claw" (2006) and "The Shakespeare Code" (2007).

Maximus Pettulian
"The Romans" (1965).

Zeus
The Myth Makers" (1965).

Doctor Caligari
"The Gunfighters" (1966).

Doctor Galloway
"The Evil of the Daleks" (1967).

The Great Wizard
"The Dæmons" (1971).

Hieronymous
"The Masque of Mandragora" (1976).

Merlin
"Battlefield" (1988).

John Doe
"Doctor Who" (1996).

Mr. Spock
"The Empty Child" (2005).

Doctor James McCrimmon
"Tooth and Claw" (2006).

Spartacus
"The Fires of Pompeii" (2008).

Chief Inspector Smith
"The Unicorn and the Wasp" (2008).

Doctor Noble
"Planet of the Ood" (2008).

Captain Troy Handsome of International Rescue
"The Lodger" (2010).

The Caretaker
"The Doctor, the Widow and the Wardrobe" (2011).

Sherlock Holmes
"The Snowmen" (2012).

Proconsol
"Nightmare in Silver" (2013).

Nicknames of the Doctor

Of course, the Doctor has also collected some interesting nicknames over the years, including:

- **Clown, Comedian, Dandy, Matchstick Man, Sandshoes, Grandad, Captain Grumpy,** and **Chinny**—all given to him by his other selves at various stages
- **Master** by K9

- **Professor** by Ace
- **Martian Boy, Spaceman,** and **Time Boy** by Donna Noble
- **Sweetie** by River Song
- **Mad Man with a Box** and **Raggedy Doctor** by Amy Pond
- **Chin Boy** by Clara
- **The Oncoming Storm** by the Daleks

Catchphrases

The Doctor has his outfit, his accessories, his TARDIS, and his companions. But what else does a Time Lord need? Yes, a catchphrase. Each regeneration has something new to say (though some do steal from others, as you will see), so here are the most notable of phrases that Gallifrey's finest like to repeat.

The First Doctor

Starting off with a tricky one here. William Hartnell was perhaps a little too severe to be wandering about space and time spouting off about the wonders around him. The First Doctor did, however, like to question all those around him with a smugly quizzical, "Hmmmm…?" on many occasions. He also rather enjoyed getting Ian Chesterton's name wrong, too.

The Second Doctor

Slightly easier for Patrick Troughton's incarnation—"When I say run, run. RUN!" was his axiom of choice. The recorder-playing alien can be heard saying it in his very first adventure, "The Power of the Daleks" (1966).

The Third Doctor

"Reverse the polarity of the neutron flow" was often thought to be this incarnation's most commonly used quote. In fact, he says it only fully on television in "The Sea Devils" (1972) and "The Five Doctors" (1983). Though, for the majority of the time, he simply reverses the polarity.

The Fourth Doctor

An easy-to-spot one here. In his opening story, "Robot," Tom Baker asks, "Would you like a jelly baby?" and would go on to repeat the question many more times. Interestingly, the Fourth Doctor makes no mention of jelly babies in his last season in the TARDIS.

Fact fans will note that he was not the first incarnation to offer the tasty treat. In "The Three Doctors" (1972–73), the Second Doctor asks, "Care for a jelly baby?" (and is also seen eating them in 1968's "The Dominators").

The Fifth Doctor

"Brave heart, Tegan," the Fifth Doctor often optimistically intoned to his Australian buddy. He would say it at least once every season he was there. And to repay the compliment, Tegan herself says, "Brave heart, Tegan," in "Resurrection of the Daleks" (1984).

The Sixth to War Doctors

Oddly, during the 1980s, catchphrases went out of fashion—much like *Doctor Who* itself. You could argue that Colin's jacket and Sylvester's question-mark pullover and umbrella were catchphrases, but verbally they don't have anything in their locker (though Colin Baker was fond of saying "I wonder" quite a lot). Paul McGann and John Hurt weren't around long enough to get their own.

The Ninth Doctor

Boom! Back with a vengeance—*Doctor Who* and the catchphrase. In his debut episode, "Rose," Christopher Eccleston can be heard exclaiming, "Fantastic!" and he didn't stop, with only three of his episodes not including it (2005's "World War Three," "The Empty Child," and "Bad Wolf").

The Tenth Doctor

David Tennant's Time Lord had a few catchphrases in his time. Who can forget "Timey-Wimey" or "I'm sorry, I'm so sorry," or even how he described everything as "Beautiful?" All classics. But, of course, the most popular and most used (by far) is "Allons-y." Take that, jelly babies!

The Eleventh Doctor

Again, during the Matt Smith era, there were a few catchphrases from the youngest of the Time Lords. But beating "Allons-y" is one of the first words uttered by the Eleventh Doctor: "Geronimo!" You can hear him exclaim it frequently during his tenure. Prizes also go to "Come along, Pond!" "Timey wimey," and "Bow ties (or whatever he is referring to at that moment) are/is cool."

The Twelfth Doctor

Um, "Kidneys"?

Dude, Where's My...TARDIS?

In the world of *Doctor Who*, we met the TARDIS before we even met the Doctor. And yet, there are some episodes—in fact, some complete stories—where the old girl is nowhere to be seen. It doesn't bear thinking about, I know, but here are those offending adventures that didn't feature *Doctor Who*'s most iconic feature, the TARDIS.

"Mission to the Unknown" (1965)

This one-part story (which acted as a prelude to "The Daleks' Master Plan") not only had the audacity not to include the TARDIS, but it also neglected to feature the Doctor or any of his companions!

"Doctor Who and the Silurians" (1970)

It would be a few years until the production team dared to forget the Time Lord's ship of choice, and it was in this Jon Pertwee eco-tale where it was ignored. To make up for it, they stuck the name of the show in the name of the episode (they wouldn't do that again for a while).

"The Sea Devils" (1972)

Just two years later in this six-parter, also featuring Pertwee, we saw the appearance of the Silurian's amphibious cousins, the "Sea Devils." The absence of the TARDIS is compensated for in a delicious scheme by the Master.

"The Sontaran Experiment" (1975)

Just a little later, with Tom Baker in charge and traveling with Sarah Jane Smith and Harry Sullivan, the gang used a transmit beam from the Nerva Beacon to Earth (thirtieth century, apparently). Pity for them, as using the TARDIS would have probably meant they wouldn't have come into contact with those nasty Sontarans.

"Genesis of the Daleks" (1975)

And, blimey, in the very next story, there was no TARDIS love either (a great disadvantage in this story, having to rely on the Gallifreyan Time Ring). Interesting that such a well-loved story (always in top 10 favorites of all time lineups) doesn't feature the Doctor's BFF. By the end of this story, fans had been without the TARDIS for eight episodes. Utterly shocking.

"Midnight" (2008)

And finally the most recent episode on this list, the David Tennant outing "Midnight." Again, the Doctor could *really* have done with the TARDIS here to get away from his rather unpleasant traveling companions. Russell T. Davies also did away with the companion (Donna Noble) in this story, along with the Doctor's voice. The fiend!

Talkin' 'Bout Regeneration

The Doctor has regenerated a few times, and sometimes question-ably, but there have been others at it, too. This graph demonstrates which decades have had the most regenerations.

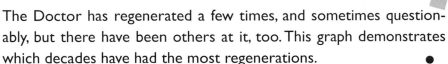

Number of Regenerations

1960s   1970s   1980s   1990s   2000s   2010s

The **sixties** were fairly straightforward, with William Hartnell regen-erating into Patrick Troughton, and then the latter regenerating into, well, no one, in "The War Games" (1969). The decade finished on quite the cliffhanger!

The **seventies** saw Jon Pertwee change into Tom Baker, and Time Lady Romana regenerate from Mary Tamm into Lalla Ward (technical-ly, she does this a few times as she tries out a few bodies, but for the purposes of this poll, we'll just count it as once).

The **eighties** ramped up change with Tom Baker morphing into Peter Davison, and he into Colin Baker. The Sixth Doctor did regenerate into the Seventh, though both were played by Sylvester McCoy during the process in "Time and the Rani" (1987).

Poor **nineties**. Just one, when McCoy regenerated into Paul McGann. (Though if you include the Comic Relief story, *The Curse of Fatal Death*, there were loads!)

Back with a bang in the **noughties**, and Time Lords took to regen-erating standing up. Ninth Doctor Christopher Eccleston bravely changed into David Tennant, while Derek Jacobi regenerated into John Simm as The Master in "Utopia" (2007). Tennant gets extra marks for regenerating into himself in "The Stolen Earth"/"Journey's End" (2008). (Should we count the Doctor's Daughter, Jenny, here? We decided against this as she didn't really regenerate, did she?)

We're only a few years into the **2010s** and yet we've seen so many regenerations. Tennant changed into Matt Smith on the very first day of the decade, River Song regenerated twice, and we saw Paul McGann, John Hurt, and Matt Smith regenerate, all in a matter of weeks!

Hats Off!

Though some incarnations of the Doctor have chosen not to wear a hat, most have. And what an interesting collection he must possess, too. Below are some of the finer moments of sartorial fun from the Time Lord.

Fez

Newer fans to *Doctor Who* might be unaware that the fez did actually make an appearance back in the 1980s, when the Seventh Doctor was visiting Windsor Castle in "Silver Nemesis" (1988). Of course, it is Matt Smith's Eleventh Doctor who made the headwear famous, first wearing one in his first season finale, "The Big Bang" (2010) (much to the bemusement of River and Amy). He would go on to wear a fez many, many more times during his era.

Fedora

Like Indiana Jones, the Doctor wasn't shy about wearing a fedora in his time. Tom Baker brandished it for most of his time on the show (with the odd exception), beaten only by his love for his scarf.

Balmoral Bonnet

Speaking of the Fourth Doctor, he did, in fact, don a Balmoral bonnet in "Terror of the Zygons" (1975) while investigating the Loch Ness Monster. Way before that, however, the Second Doctor also wore one, while in Scotland, in "The Highlanders" (1967).

Deerstalker

Tom Baker again and, while auditioning for Sherlock Holmes, his curly head of hair was topped off with a deerstalker in "The Talons of Weng-Chiang" (1977). The Eleventh Doctor, posing as the Baker Street sleuth, also wore one in "The Snowmen" (2012).

Stetson

Sticking with Matt Smith's Time Lord, his love for headgear (much like Patrick Troughton's Doctor) showed no bounds as he entertained everyone by wearing a Stetson in 2011's "The Impossible Astronaut" (given to him in "Closing Time"). Unsurprisingly, he also fashioned one in the Wild West story "A Town Called Mercy" (2012). Going back in time though we find that the Eighth Doctor was not a fan of the Stetson, deciding against it when discovering a Wild Bill Hickok costume in the 1996 TV Movie.

Astrakhan

Ever the oddball and contrarian, the First Doctor's headwear of choice was an Astrakhan, first seen in the opening episode, "An Unearthly Child" (1963).

Stovepipe

Likewise, the First Doctor's successor was also fond of rather outlandish hats. After regenerating, he picked out the most unusual stovepipe in "The Power of the Daleks" (1966). Though Troughton wouldn't stick with it for long, choosing to remain hatless despite his continuing obsession (often he would say, "I would like a hat like that.").

Panama Hat

The Fifth and Seventh Doctors regularly wore Panamas on their travels, though the former would usually roll it up and stick it in his pocket. whilst the latter would constantly wear it (even to his "death"). But fact fans will also note that William Hartnell's First Doctor donned one whilst in Egypt during "The Daleks' Master Plan" (1965–66).

Of Course, We Didn't Forget...

- **Viking Helmet** (the Fourth Doctor)
- **Bowler** and **Top Hat** (the Eleventh Doctor)
- **Straw Hat** (the Tenth Doctor)
- **Trilby** (the Third Doctor)

It's Bigger on the Inside!

The phrase "bigger on the inside" has become synonymous with *Doctor Who* and, more specifically, the interior of the TARDIS, usually when a new companion enters it. You might be surprised to learn that those four iconic words were barely used in the series' classic run from 1963 to 1989, while its usage has more than doubled since the 2005 return.

"The War Games" (1969)

Incredibly, it was almost six years before the immortal phrase was uttered, and even then it wasn't inside the ship. Companion Zoe said, "That thing must be bigger inside than outside, just like the TARDIS," on the appearance of soldiers emerging from a SIDRAT (a TARDIS-like ship used by the War Lords).

"Colony in Space" (1971)

The first genuine BOTI™ moment from a companion comes when companion Jo Grant sees inside for the first time (in her fourth story): "I don't believe it! It's bigger inside than out!"

"The Three Doctors" (1972)

The Doctor uses it himself in the first multi-Doctor story, somewhat dejectedly saying to Sergeant Benton, "Aren't you going to say it—that it's bigger on the inside than it is on the outside. Everybody else does." Ever the wag, his UNIT buddy replies, "It's pretty obvious, isn't it? Anyway, nothing to do with you surprises me anymore, Doctor." There's no pleasing some people.

"The Robots of Death" (1977)

A semi-mention here in this Tom Baker classic when companion Leela demands, "Explain to me how this TARDIS is larger on the inside than the out." It's not "bigger," but we'll give it to her anyway.

"Keeper of Traken" (1981)

The next companion, Nyssa, inquires, "But why is it so much bigger inside than it is outside?" in her debut story. Unfortunately, she asks Adric, who retorts, "The Doctor told me that was because it was dimensionally transcendental."

"Resurrection of the Daleks" (1984)

Over a decade after Gallifrey's finest first used the phrase, the Doctor wheels it out to explain to Dalek spy Stien, "It's bigger inside than out." Unfortunately for Stien, he couldn't stand the confusion in his mind.

"Timelash" (1985)

Herbert (who would turn out to be author H.G. Wells), while gazing upon the TARDIS's delights, appreciatively articulated, "Just look at this place. I can't believe it. Do you know it's actually bigger inside than it is on the outside?" To which the Sixth Doctor simply said, "I know."

"Dragonfire" (1987)

The last you'll hear of it in the classic run is in Mel's last appearance, and Ace's first. The former explains the TARDIS to the latter: "Well, it's bigger on the inside than the outside." At least Mel was good for something.

"Rose" (2005)

The return of *Doctor Who* saw the return of the phrase, and just look how many times it pops up in its first year back. Not quite getting it after the shock of entering the TARDIS, it was Rose who proffered, "The inside's bigger than the outside?"

"Aliens of London" (2005)

Shortly after, Rose's mum, Jackie, tells a police officer, who was actually a Slithcen, about the Doctor's mode of travel: "It was bigger on the inside. I don't know. What do I know about spaceships?"

"The Doctor Dances" (2005)

Captain Jack Harkness, who must have seen the odd and unusual thing in his time, was even left to remark on joining the TARDIS crew: "Much bigger on the inside."

"Doomsday" (2006)

Not talking about his TARDIS wife here, but the Doctor refers to the Genesis Ark as "bigger on the inside." That's Time Lord science for you!

"The Runaway Bride" (2006)

In the very next episode (and the middle of three which all use the phrase), David Tennant's Tenth Doctor tries to soothe Catherine Tate's Donna Noble, who's freaking out over the alien ship, calmly informing her, "It's bigger on the inside, that's all." As we will see later, the Chiswick temp soon gets used to it.

"Smith and Jones" (2007)

And completing the trilogy is this nugget from the suitably impressed Martha Jones: "It's like a box with that room just rammed in. It's bigger on the inside." Ever cool, Ten responds nonchalantly, "Is it? I hadn't noticed."

"Partners in Crime" (2008)

On her reunion with the Doctor and the TARDIS, Donna Noble was told by the Time Lord, "It's bigger on the inside than it is on the outside." Unimpressed, she replied, "Oh, I know that bit. Although frankly, you could turn the heating up."

"The Sontaran Stratagem" (2008)

Sticking with Donna, she tells her granddad, Wilf, "It's bigger on the inside." More from him later.

"The Waters of Mars" (2009)

In the Tenth Doctor's penultimate story, Mia, recently saved from the doomed Bowie Base One on Mars, stumbles out of the TARDIS in horror exclaiming, "What is that thing? It's bigger. I mean, it's bigger on the inside. Who the hell are you?" Just goes to show that the Doctor's way of life isn't a positive experience for everyone.

"The End of Time" (2010)

Back to everyone's favorite old-timer, Wilf! When Donna's granddad finally gets a journey in the TARDIS, the Tenth Doctor beams, looking pleased with himself, and says, "Bigger on the inside. Do you like it?" Wilf remarks, in a very Donna fashion, "I thought it'd be cleaner."

"The Vampires of Venice" (2010)

The Eleventh Doctor, concerned for Rory's mental well-being, sympathized, "It's a lot to take in, isn't it?" Sadly, for the Gallifreyan, Mr. Williams wasn't taken aback, leading Matt Smith's Doctor to grumble, "I like the bit when someone says it's bigger on the inside. I always look forward to that." Aw, bless.

"Amy's Choice" (2010)

Stating the obvious, the aforementioned Rory says, "Okay, we're in a spaceship that's bigger on the inside than the outside." Nicely noticed, Williams.

"A Christmas Carol" (2010)

In a first for *Doctor Who*, two different actors playing the same character get to complete the phrase "It's bigger on...the inside". Kazran Sardick starts off as his older self, and then finishes the phrase with his younger self. Timey-wimey, and all that.

"The Impossible Astronaut" (2011)

Experiencing the shock of the TARDIS interior for the first time, the Doctor's CIA buddy, Canton, notices wide-eyed, "It's bigger on the inside."

"The Curse of the Black Spot" (2011)

Likewise, when the Gallifreyan's new pirate chum, Captain Avery, enters, mystified and bewildered, he's rendered speechless. Just as well, as the mouthy Time Lord informs him, "Let me stop you there. Bigger on the inside."

"The Doctor's Wife" (2011)

On becoming human, as Idris, she would announce, "So much bigger on the inside!" And she should know.

"Let's Kill Hitler" (2011)

A young River Song, in the form of Mels, gets excited before she's even entered the TARDIS. "Is that the phone box? The bigger on the inside phone box?" she coos, upon seeing it.

"The Snowmen" (2012)

In a remarkable first, and recognized as such by the Doctor, Clara identifies the dimensional anomaly slightly different to everyone else. "It's smaller on the outside," she decides. Well spotted, you clever girl!

"The Bells of Saint John" (2013)

The modern-day version of Clara would have a more surprised reaction. With more pressing matters at hand, the Eleventh Doctor tells her, "Yes, it's a spaceship. Yes, it's bigger on the inside. Now, I don't have time to talk about it." To which Miss Oswald repeats in awe, "Bigger on the inside. Actually bigger." Now, *that's* a proper BOTI™ moment.

The Name of the Doctor (2013)

On explaining why there was a huge TARDIS on Trenzalore, Matt Smith's Doctor said, "They used to call it a size leak. All the bigger on the inside starts leaking to the outside."

The Day of the Doctor (2013)

Another first here as two different incarnations of the Doctor get a piece of the action. Whilst gazing upon a "3-D painting," Eleven describes it as "Time Lord art. Bigger on the inside." And then, when showing off to Elizabeth I, Ten boasts, "There you go, your Majesty, what did I tell you? Bigger on the inside."

The Time of the Doctor (2013)

And finally, and in his final episode, the Eleventh Doctor has a chat with a young Trenzalorian boy, Barnable, and asks him how his father's barn is, to which the reply comes, "You've fixed the leak all right, but he says it's bigger on the inside now." Naughty Doctor!

Rarely Seen TARDIS Rooms

The console room, for sure, is where it's all at for the Doctor and his traveling companions, but there are other rooms in the TARDIS. Find the rarities below.

Cloister Room

The Fourth Doctor's final story, "Logopolis" (1981), featured the first use of the Cloister Bell and the first look at its room. It was pretty much like any other TARDIS room in the eighties—too bright and creamy with roundels, though with the addition of pillars and vines. It was some time before it appeared again, albeit in a more Gothic cathedral style in the 1996 TV Movie (with bats for good measure).

Swimming Pool

The Fourth Doctor six-parter, "The Invasion of Time" (1978), is famous, really, for just one thing: the appearance of the TARDIS swimming pool. No expense was spent on displaying the luxury of the Time Lord's ship in all its tacky seventies glory. Eagle-eyed viewers will also have spotted a glimpse of it in "Journey to the Centre of the TARDIS" (2013), though it did look rather more attractive in that episode. Oddly, the Eleventh Doctor deleted the swimming pool in "The Doctor's Wife" (2010), so he must have made another.

Library

The Twelfth Doctor, obviously a reader, included part of the library in his console room, much like the Seventh Doctor did in the 1996 TV Movie. In "The Eleventh Hour" (2010), the Gallifreyan revealed that the swimming pool had fallen into the library, while "Journey to the Centre of the TARDIS" (2013) saw companion Clara discover the vast room, and a certain book, *The History of the Time War*.

Art Gallery

Blink and you'll miss a chance to see the Doctor's love of art in "The Invasion of Time" (1978).

Storage Room

Another one featured in "Journey to the Centre of the TARDIS," where Clara discovered lots of the Time Lord's old junk.

Bedrooms

During the very early years, we saw some of the rooms where companions such as Barbara, Susan, and Vicki slept, but it wasn't until Romana when we saw another bedroom again. The eighties, however,

was a bedfest—with Nyssa, Adric, Tegan, Peri, and even Turlough showing off their chambers. All bedrooms have been jettisoned (in the case
of Romana) or deleted (with the exception of the never-seen Rory
and Amy bedroom). But, the real question is, where does the Doctor
sleep…?

Zero Room

Well, to answer the question—where does the Doctor sleep?—possibly here. While the Fifth Doctor was undergoing some post-regenerative stress, he took a nap in this room in "Castrovalva" (1982). It didn't
last long, though, and the room was destroyed shortly after, giving birth
to the Zero Cabinet.

Secondary Console Room

Season 14 saw the introduction of this beautiful Jules Verne take on
the TARDIS Console Room. Engulfed in luscious wood paneling and
stained-glass windows, the room was introduced in "The Masque of
Mandragora" (1976) and was the home to the touching good-bye
scene between Sarah Jane and the Fourth Doctor. Sadly, the room was
only used in a few stories.

Botanical House

Repeat-offender "The Invasion of Time" again. A poor Sontaran came
to a sticky end in here, as a huge carnivorous plant decided to chomp
down on him.

Boot Cupboard

Though described by the Fourth Doctor as a "not very interesting"
boot cupboard, according to Sarah Jane in "The Masque of Mandragora" (1976), this was an enormous room. Indeed, the quick glimpse
we got as viewers suggested this was an elegant English
drawing room of some description. The Doctor has always been modest.

7 Unseen TARDIS Rooms

As we know, the TARDIS is a big old place, with lots of rooms to hide in and get up to all sorts of adventures. But there are a number of rooms mentioned though never seen. Here are some of the more notable.

Kitchen

Though never broadcast on television, "Shada" (1979), the infamous Fourth Doctor story written by the late great Douglas Adams, revealed that Romana had "never known" her fellow Gallifreyan to use the TARDIS kitchen. During "The Curse of the Black Spot" (2011), the Eleventh Doctor welcomed Captain Avery into the TARDIS, upon which he directed him to the whereabouts of the kitchen ("that way"). In "The Snowmen" (2012), one of Clara's first questions about the Time Lord's ship was, "Is there a kitchen?" Bemused, the Doctor admitted that this question had not been asked before.

Squash Court

In fact, there are at least six, currently. In "The Doctor's Wife" (2011), the Eleventh Doctor burned up Squash Court 7 in order to speed up the TARDIS. He also got rid of the…

Scullery Room

What's a scullery room, you ask? It's a room used for cleaning dishes and clothes. Weird, because we never see him eat in the TARDIS, and he rarely changes outfits.

Garage

Both "The Idiot's Lantern" (2006) and "The Bells of Saint John" (2013) reveal the Doctor's love for motorcycles. In the latter, after driving out on to London's Southbank, the Eleventh Doctor tells Clara, "Just popping back to the garage!" Presumably, this is where Clara's bike ended up in "The Day of the Doctor" (2013).

Sick Bay

Those paying close attention in "Cold Blood" (2011) will know that the sick bay is "up the stairs, left, then left again."

Bathroom

According to "The Curse of the Black Spot," when the Eleventh Doctor brought Captain Avery aboard, there were a "choice" of bathrooms. Just as well really, the Doctor does like an entourage.

Cricket Pitch

Never referred to, but why else would the Doctor store bats and cricket whites?

The Name's Smith, John Smith

To keep his mystique and secrecy, the Doctor uses an actual name to conduct his business, and more often than not he uses John Smith. Below you'll find all the stories in which it has been used by either the Time Lord or his companions on his behalf.

"The Wheel in Space" (1968)

"The War Games" (1969)

"Spearhead from Space" (1970)

"Inferno" (1970)

"The Time Warrior" (1973)

"Doctor Who" (1996)

"School Reunion" (2006)

"Smith and Jones" (2007)

"Human Nature" (2007)

"Partners in Crime" (2008)

"The Unicorn and the Wasp" (2008)

"Midnight" (2008)

"Journey's End" (2008)

"The Next Doctor" (2008)

"The Almost People" (2011)

"The Crimson Horror" (2013)

Honorable Mention

Not spoken aloud but seen, the name John Smith is brandished on the following:

- **"The Empty Child"** (2005): on psychic paper
- **"The Vampires of Venice"** (2010): on his library card (which featured a picture of William Hartnell, suggesting that the First Doctor went by this nom de plume)

Of Course, We Didn't Forget...

In the first episode, **"An Unearthly Child"** (1963), granddaughter Susan was seen to be a big fan of the British band John Smith and the Common Men ("They've gone from nineteen to two," she beams), though, as Ian Chesterton pointed out in that episode, John Smith was, in fact, the stage name of the "Honorable" Aubrey Waites.

Witty Little Knitter

The Fourth Doctor was perhaps best known for his immense and lengthy scarf. Tom Baker is synonymous with it, but it wasn't just a sartorial choice—it came in handy in saving his skin and defeating baddies. Check out some uses of the scarf that may have passed you by.

Unsuccessful Guard Distractor

In just his second outing, "The Ark in Space" (1975), the Doctor was already referring to it as his "faithful old scarf." In a bid to pull a lever to disable the Nerva Station's auto-guard, it got zapped. Poor thing.

Puzzle Measurer

Later that year, the wide-eyed Gallifreyan used it to measure what he referred to as a "Chinese Puzzle" in "Pyramids of Mars." The Doctor calculated, "A hundred and twenty point three centimeters, multiplied by the binary figure ten zero zero. That's a hundred and sixty two point four centimeters, correct?" Show off. He also used it to lasso one of his armed assailants earlier in the story.

Enemy Tripper

Handy for a quick getaway or attack, the Time Lord used the scarf to stave off execution in "The Masque of Mandragora" (1976); to trip Eldrad down a chasm in "The Hand of Fear" (1976), with the help of Sarah Jane; and in his finale, "Logopolis" (1981), to also trip his enemy, the Master.

Rope

The scarf was functional in many ways for the Doctor. It kept him warm and tripped multiple enemies, but it also got him out of tight situations. His lengthy accessory helped out in both "The Deadly Assassin" (1976) and "The Stones of Blood" (1978) when a cliff face proved hazardous first for him and then for Romana. In "The Creature from the Pit" (1979), Tom Baker had to climb out of that titular pit after reading *Everest in Easy Stages*—though unsuccessfully, it should be said. The cheeky Time Lord even used his scarf as a leash for K9 in "The Invisible Enemy" (1977).

Framing Tool

The first story of the eighties saw a more subdued and somber Fourth Doctor, and his outfit reflected this accordingly with its burgundy tones. Gone, too, were the colorful bars on his scarf, but that did not mean it wasn't a prominent feature anymore. Oh no. A corpse was found in "The Leisure Hive" (1980) and the cause of the murder was believed to have been the scarf, to which the Gallifreyan retorted, "Arrest the scarf, then!" As it transpired, the scarf was a plant by someone hoping to frame the time-and-space traveler.

Words and Relative Explanations in Space

Surprisingly, given how many people know what TARDIS stands for, the phrase hasn't been used that much since 1963. Apart from a spurt of repetitions in the William Hartnell years, its usage is pretty sparse with Troughton, Pertwee, both Bakers, and Smith not saying it all! So, word fans, here all the uses of "Time And Relative Dimension In Space" in *Doctor Who*, including who said it and in what story.

Susan in "An Unearthly Child" (1963)
The Fifth Doctor in "Frontios" (1984)
The Eighth Doctor in the TV Movie (1996)
The Ninth Doctor in "Rose" (2005)
The Tenth Doctor in "Smith and Jones" (2007)
Rose in "Turn Left" (2008)
Idris in "The Doctor's Wife" (2011)
Susan in "Journey to the Centre of the TARDIS" (2013)

However, to confuse matters (and as a *Doctor Who* fan you should be used to that by now), TARDIS has been explained as "Time And Relative Dimensions In Space"—even by some Doctors. Here are those instances.

Vicki in "The Time Meddler" (1965)
The First Doctor in "The Daleks' Master Plan" (1966)
The First Doctor in "The Massacre of St. Bartholomew's Eve" (1966)
Dodo in "The War Machines" (1966)
Zoe in "The Wheel In Space" (1968)
Zoe in "The War Games" (1969)
K9 in "The Creature from the Pit" (1979)
Adric in "Four to Doomsday" (1982)
The Seventh Doctor in "Delta and the Bannermen" (1987)

Honorable Mention

And, of course, full marks to **Jackson Lake** who came up with his own acronym for TARDIS—Tethered Aerial Release Developed in Style—for his big balloon in 2008's "The Next Doctor."

Classic Companions and Friends' First Words

Can you guess which companions and friends of the Doctor uttered these first words between 1963 and 1989 in *Doctor Who*? For the answers, see page 250.

1. "There's a wee drop left yet."

2. "Aren't you jealous, Father?"

3. "Passport."

4. "Crude, heavy and inefficient."

5. "Was all that nonsense out there really necessary? Identity passes? Guards? I was even searched."

6. "Stay where you are! You real?"

7. "Oh, I'm sorry, Miss Wright. I didn't hear you coming in. Aren't they fabulous?"

8. "Yes, Professor?"

9. "Where's the telephone?"

10. "Don't beg, Tomas. What I said was the truth."

11. "Twenty three, twenty four, twenty five."

12. "The mistake's in your wallet, not my arithmetic."

Classic Quotes

Here you'll find some of the very best quotes from 1963 through 1989—and all you have to do is identify the character and the story! For the answers, see page 250.

1. "A straight line may be the shortest distance between two points but it is by no means the most interesting."

2. "There's no point in being grown up if you can't be childish sometimes."

3. "But I don't know, rocket fire at long range, it's… I don't know, somehow it lacks that personal touch."

4. "I'm not helping you, officially. And if anyone happens to ask whether I made any material difference to the welfare of this planet, you can tell them I came and went like a summer cloud."

5. "You know, I am so constantly outwitting the opposition, I tend to forget the delights and satisfaction of the arts, the gentle art of fisticuffs."

6. "As long as he does the job, he can wear what face he likes."

7. "Our lives are different to anybody else's. That's the exciting thing, that nobody in the universe can do what we're doing."

8. "We're talking about the Daleks, the most evil creatures ever invented, you must destroy them! You must complete your mission for the Time Lords!"

9. "Your species has the most amazing capacity for self-deception, matched only by its ingenuity when trying to destroy itself."

10. "Change? What change? There is no change…no time, no rhyme, no place for space, nothing! Nothing but the grinding engines of the universe, the crushing boredom of eternity!"

Famous Last Words: Classic *Who*

Here you'll find some of the very best dying words from between 1963 and 1989—and all you have to do is identify the character and the story! (Hint: these are in chronological order.) For the answers, see page 250

1. "We must survive! We must survive!"

2. "I hurt! Help me! I am burning! My brain is on fire! Help me!"

3. "Good-bye, Vira…"

4. "I shall kill you all now, but first I have more important tasks to perform."

5. "You are insane, Davros!"

6. "Soon I shall join my ancestors. Already I can see them. They walk to greet me from the Palace of Jade. They are smiling and carry gifts of food and flowers. Now I cross the golden bridge of the gods."

7. "You and your kind are nothing but parasites. You're dependent upon us for the air you breathe and the food you eat. We have only one use for you."

8. "Now I'll never know if I was right…"

9. "Salateen, hold me…"

10. "Please, Doctor. Kill me."

Famous Last Words: New *Who*

Here you'll find some of the very best dying words from 2005 on-ward—and all you have to do is identify the character and the story! (Hint: these are in chronological order.) For the answers, see page 250.

1. "Whaddya gonna do? Sucker me to de—"

2. "With respect, sir. The human race is taking its first step towards the stars, but we are like children compared to you. Children who need help. Children who need compassion. I beg of you now, show that compassion."

3. "I committed treason for you, but now my wife will remember me with honor!"

4. "You bad dog!"

5. "I shall never die. The thought of me is forever—in the bleeding hearts of men, in their vanity and obsessions and lust. Nothing shall ever destroy me, nothing!"

6. "I did my duty for Queen and Country. I did my duty. I did my duty. Oh, God. I did my duty."

7. "Sontar-HA!"

8. "Never forget, Doctor, you did this. I name you. Forever, you are the destroyer of the worlds!"

9. Tell me, Doctor. Can your conscience carry the weight of another dead race? Remember us. Dream of us."

10. "Thank you, Doctor. I have to face the souls of those I've wronged. Perhaps they will be kind."

New Series Quotes

Here you'll find some of the very best quotes from *Doctor Who* (2005 onward)—and all you have to do is identify the character and the story! For the answers, see page 251.

1. "You want weapons? We're in a library! Books! The best weapons in the world!"

2. "The past is another country. 1987's just the Isle of Wight."

3. "Well, they're certainly not random space debris. They're too perfectly formed for that. Are they extraterrestrial in origin? Well, you'll have to ask a better man than me."

4. "Do you know, in nine hundred years of time and space, I've never met anyone who wasn't important."

5. "When you run with the Doctor, it feels like it will never end. But however hard you try, you can't run forever. Everybody knows that everybody dies, and nobody knows it like the Doctor. But I do think that all the skies of all the worlds might just turn dark, if he ever, for one moment, accepts it."

6. "There's a man who will never let us down. And not even an army can get in the way."

7. "The Doctor showed me a better way of living your life. You know he showed you, too. That you don't just give up. You don't just let things happen. You make a stand. You say no. You have the guts to do what's right when everyone else just runs away, and I just can't."

8. "But what I wanted to say is, you know, when you're a kid, they tell you it's all, grow up, get a job, get married, get a house, have a kid, and that's it. But the truth is, the world is so much stranger than that. It's so much darker, and so much madder. And so much better."

9. "Two minutes to Belgium!"

10. "Listen, Sister, you might have eyes on the back of your hands but you'll have eyes in the back of your head by the time I'm finished with you."

New Series Companions and Friends' First Words

Now it's the turn of the new series companions and friends of the Doctor and their first words in Doctor Who. Be wary, though, it is not as straightforward as it seems… For the answers, see page 251.

1. "Bye!"

2. "Oh! Who are you?"

3. "You're up early. What's happening?"

4. "Dear Santa. Thank you for the dolls and pencils and the fish."

5. "Angie? Is the internet working? Trying to phone the helpline, they won't answer."

6. "Excellent bottom."

7. "Oh ho, scared!"

8. "I've been phoning your mobile. You could've been dead. It's on the news and everything."

9. "Day three six three. The terror continues. Also, made another…"

10. "Thank you, Parker. I won't be needing you again tonight."

11. "Did you make this snowman?"

12. "You did not indicate a preference."

The Doctors' First Words

Do you remember the first words uttered by each incarnation of the Doctor? For the answers, see page 251.

1. You're expecting someone else?

2. Doctor no more.

3. Run!

4. What are you doing here?

5. Legs. I've still got legs!

6. Stop. Stop. Concentrate on one thing. One thing.

7. Hello. Okay. Ooo, new teeth. That's weird. So, where was I? Oh, that's right. Barcelona.

8. No, no, Mel. That was a nice nap. Now, down to business.

9. Shoes. Must find my shoes.

10. I, oh.

11. Who am I? Who am I? Who am I?

12. [MUMBLES] Brigadier, there's nothing to worry about. The brontosaurus is large and placid.

13. Kidneys! I've got new kidneys. I don't like the color.

The Doctors' Last Words

Can you identify the last words uttered by each incarnation of the Doctor? No cheating! For the answers, see page 251.

1. "Stop, you're making me giddy! No, you can't do this to me! No!"

2. "Carrot juice, carrot juice, carrot juice."

3. "A tear, Sarah Jane? No, don't cry. While there's life, there's…"

4. "Rose, before I go, I just want to tell you, you were fantastic. Absolutely fantastic. And do you know what? So was I."

5. "Ah, yes. Thank you. It's good. Keep warm."

6. "I will always remember when the Doctor was me."

7. "Physician, heal thyself."

8. "Adric?"

9. "Wearing a bit thin. I hope the ears are a bit less conspicuous this time."

10. "I've got to stop him."

11. "It's the end. But the moment has been prepared for."

12. "I don't want to go."

Who Said What?

A dozen actors have played the Time Lord and all have been interviewed at length about their time on the show. But can you identify who, out of those twelve men, said the following about *Doctor Who.* For the answers, see page 251.

12. "*Doctor Who,* like time, cannot stand still. It must always move and change."

11. "I was so pleased to be offered *Doctor Who.* To me, kids are the greatest audience, and the greatest critics, in the world."

10. "I loved playing him, and I loved taking part in the basic essence and message of the series, which is 'It's a short life, seize it and live it as fully as you can.'"

9. "I think *Dr. Who* was more or less me. The first one I did, I played for laughs."

8. "The great thing about *Doctor Who* is that everyone has their place. We can happily co-exist, and we all have various things going for us. I could move quicker than most of the classic Doctors."

7. "There's sometimes something quite adolescent about him. So if you can get a guy who's sixty-odd to play him, it's even more pronounced. It's like Lear."

6. "What annoyed me most was the small vocal group of so-called *Doctor Who* fans. They annoyed me immensely."

5. "It was a lovely part, I loved doing it and the family audience liked me very much in it, and I regretted leaving it very much, but again you can't stay in one job forever."

4. "It's an iconic part of our culture. My granddad knows about it, my dad knows about it…it has the iconic status of Robin Hood or Sherlock Holmes [has]."

3. "I can understand that some people would miss that message and just see the violence. The good thing about *Doctor Who* is that it does carry messages. Behind every story, if you look for it, it's usually making some other point."

2. "I think it's just stories for everyone and it appeals to children as much as everyone else. It's extraordinary the kind of stretch of age ranges that the show seems to attract. The people who come up to you in the street, it's as often an old lady as an eight-year-old kid, which is lovely."

1. "*Doctor Who*'s longevity is because there is no other show quite like it."

Classic Companions and Friends' First Words (page 240)

1. Jamie
2. Nyssa
3. Tegan
4. Turlough
5. Liz Shaw
6. Steven
7. Susan
8. Sarah Jane Smith
9. Dodo
10. Leela
11. Mel
12. Ace

Classic Quotes (page 241)

1. The Third Doctor, "The Time Warrior" (1973–74)
2. The Fourth Doctor, "Robot" (1974–75)
3. The Master, "Frontier In Space" (1973)
4. The Fifth Doctor, "Frontios" (1984)
5. The First Doctor, "The Romans" (1965)
6. The Brigadier, "The Three Doctors" (1972–73)
7. The Second Doctor, "The Tomb of the Cybermen" (1967)
8. Sarah Jane Smith, "Genesis of the Daleks" (1975)
9. The Seventh Doctor, "Remembrance of the Daleks" (1988)
10. The Sixth Doctor, "The Twin Dilemma" (1984)

Famous Last Words: Classic *Who* (page 242)

1. The Cyber-Controller, "The Tomb of the Cybermen" (1967)
2. The Great One, "Planet of the Spiders" (1974)
3. Noah, "The Ark in Space" (1975)
4. Stryre, "The Sontaran Experiment" (1975)
5. Gharman, "Genesis of the Daleks" (1975)
6. Li Hsen Chang, "The Talons of Weng-Chiang" (1977)
7. Harrison Chase, "The Seeds of Doom" (1976)
8. Adric, "Earthshock" (1982)
9. Sharaz Jek, "The Caves of Androzani" (1984)
10. Gustave Lytton, "Attack of the Cybermen" (1985

Famous Last Words: New *Who* (page 243)

1. Simmons, "Dalek" (2005)
2. Daniel Llewellyn, "The Christmas Invasion" (2005)
3. Robert MacLeish, "Tooth and Claw" (2006)
4. Mr. Finch, "School Reunion" (2006)
5. The Beast, "The Satan Pit" (2006)
6. Yvonne Hartman, "Doomsday" (2006)
7. Luke Rattigan, "The Poison Sky" (2008)
8. Davros, "Journey's End" (2008)
9. Rosanna Calvierri, "The Vampires of Venice" (2010)
10. Kahler-Jex, "A Town Called Mercy" (2012)

New Series Quotes (page 244)

1. The Tenth Doctor, "Tooth & Claw" (2006)
2. The Ninth Doctor, "Father's Day" (2005)
3. Professor Brian Cox, "The Power of Three" (2012)
4. The Eleventh Doctor, "A Christmas Carol" (2010)
5. River Song, "Forest of the Dead" (2008)
6. Amy Pond, "A Good Man Goes to War" (2011)
7. Rose Tyler, "The Parting of the Ways" (2005)
8. Elton Pope, "Love & Monsters" (2006)

New Series Companion and Friends' First Words (page 245)

1. Rose Tyler
2. Donna Noble
3. Martha Jones
4. Amelia Pond
5. Clara ("The Bells of Saint John")
6. Captain Jack Harkness
7. Wilf
8. Mickey
9. Oswin Oswald
10. Vastra
11. Clara ("The Snowmen")
12. Handles

The Doctors' First Words (page 246)

1. The Sixth Doctor
2. The War Doctor
3. The Ninth Doctor
4. The First Doctor
5. The Eleventh Doctor
6. The Second Doctor
7. The Tenth Doctor
8. The Seventh Doctor
9. The Third Doctor
10. The Fifth Doctor
11. The Eighth Doctor
12. The Fourth Doctor
13. The Twelfth Doctor

The Doctors' Last Words (page 247)

1. Second Doctor
2. Sixth Doctor
3. Third Doctor
4. Ninth Doctor
5. First Doctor
6. Eleventh Doctor
7. Eighth Doctor
8. Fifth Doctor
9. War Doctor
10. Seventh Doctor
11. Fourth Doctor
12. Tenth Doctor

Who Said What? (page 248)

12. Peter Capaldi in 1974
11. William Hartnell in 1964
10. Christopher Eccleston in 2005
9. Jon Pertwee in 1990
8. Peter Davison in 2013
7. Paul McGann in 2004
6. Sylvester McCoy in 1988
5. Patrick Troughton in 1985
4. Matt Smith in 2009
3. Colin Baker in 1986
2. David Tennant in 2007
1. Tom Baker in 2013

About the Author

CAMERON K. McEWAN is the author of *The Who's Who of Doctor Who* (Race Point Publishing, 2014) and the man behind *Blogtor Who* (www.blogtorwho.com), a fan site dedicated to *Doctor Who*. Started in 2008, *Blogtor Who* is now one of the most popular *Doctor Who* blogs in the world, on some days receiving over 80,000 page views. Its Twitter account currently has over 50,000 followers.

Due to the site's success and popularity, Cameron makes appearances at conventions across Europe, hosting panels and interviews with *Doctor Who* personalities in front of and behind the camera, including Matt Smith, Steven Moffat, Mark Gatiss, and Murray Gold. He also makes the odd television appearance on the BBC and in the United States.

While studying film at the University of Aberdeen, Cameron obtained a first-class degree and worked alongside maverick filmmakers such as Alex Cox and Raul Ruiz. In 2014, he put these skills to use with the release of the critically acclaimed *Who's Changing: An Adventure in Time with Fans*, a feature-length documentary about *Doctor Who* fans that has been screened at film festivals in North America and the UK.

Cameron also writes for websites such as *Den of Geek*, *CultBox*, and *Metro* and is a regular entertainment contributor for BBC London.

He lives in London with his seven trousers.

Dedication

For my dad, Angus—for his constant support.

Acknowledgments

Thanks to Murray Gold, Eamonn "Macbeth" Dunne, and Matthew "Malcolm" McFetridge, for great list suggestions!; Edward Russell, for clarification; Emrys and Katie Matthews, Mark Machado, Blair Mowat, Lisa Gifford, and Elisar Cabrera; Simon Brew and Will Martin, for letting me write for their websites; Richard Starkings and Caitlin Holmes, for casting me in her play; Peter "Is a Real Person" Harness, Sebastian J. Brook, Dr. Alan Marcus, Joe Coutts, Kevin Jon Davies, Nick Fraser, Gemma-May "English Rose" Bowles and William "Bristol Bill" Baltyn, Peter Halpin, Chris "Upset Because Camsy Is a Tory" Chapman, Ed "Politics & Tennis" Stradling, Neil "The Pipe" Bushnell, John Matthews, Mel Keable, Jamie "Nice Sermon Vicar" Cowan, Alix and Malcom McKenzie, Sarika Sharma, Andrew Fllard, Michael Snooze, Alun Preece, Ciara McGrath, Gavin Dunbar, Sami Kelsh, Reetu "Deetoo" Kabra, Matt Nicholls, Chris Allen, Stan "And Deliver" Barker, and to everyone who voted "No" in the Scottish Referendum—you chose wisely.

About the Illustrator

Andrew Skilleter has been professionally involved with *Doctor Who* for thirty-five years, primarily between 1979 and 1995. His work includes the iconic "The Five Doctors" *RadioTimes* cover, dozens of book covers, including forty-nine for the Target series and related books, BBC video covers, books, calendars, prints, and other merchandise. This led him to working closely with the show's producer, John Nathan-Turner, in the 1980s. His involvement included a long liaison with the BBC, producing twenty-four distinctive video covers for the *Doctor Who* series, the collector's Tardis and Dalek tins, and other genre titles. Special projects included the exterior of the BBC USA Exhibition Trailer. His first *Doctor Who* book for many years, *The Who's Who of Doctor Who* was published in January 2014, and he continues to supply *Doctor Who* cover artwork for BBC Audio.

Andrew studied art and graphic design in Bournemouth, but he considers himself largely self-taught, studying the work of his early illustration heroes in addition to new influences. He has had a wide-ranging illustration career since the 1970s, embracing many areas from publishing and music to numerous other genres, including artwork for *The Chronicles of Narnia* BBC radio collection and official *Star Wars* merchandise.

His *Doctor Who* books include *Blacklight: The Doctor Who Art of Andrew Skilleter* (1995) that showcased a diverse selection of his professional *Who* work; the classic *Cybermen* book with David Banks, voted one of the best ever *Doctor Who* books; and *Doctor Who: Monsters*.

He lives in the English countryside in a Hansel and Gretel–style house with his wife, artist and writer Patricia Papps (www.patriciapapps.com) and continues to do commissions, both professionally and privately and developing new digital work which can be seen at

http://doxydiva.com His main website is www.andrewskilleter.com and for news and information, follow him on Facebook at http://www.facebook.com/artofandrewskilleter.

This painting doesn't belong here. Not in this time or place.

Aknowledgments

With this, my second book with Cameron K. McEwan and Race Point Publishing, I was determined at the outset that the art should be ambitious—and *fun*! My vision for the work was for it to be celebratory, as well as emotional with the "wow" factor. My editor wanted the content to reflect primarily the new series of *Doctor Who*, and I was more than happy to embrace this and mine the rich seam of visual content that it has delivered to us over the recent years, courtesy of the *Who Crew* at Cardiff. Not that the show's origins are excluded—far from it. The classic series is the foundation, the Garden of Eden, from which all else has grown. I was there and did my first professional *Doctor Who* book cover in 1979. But I'm not the serpent…I hope.

I would like to pay tribute to my editor, Jeannine Dillon at Race Point Publishing, to whom we all owe our gratitude for the vision in initiating the *Who's Who of Doctor Who* and now this even more ambitious volume, *Unofficial Doctor Who: The Big Book of Lists*. She put her trust and faith in me, allowing me full rein to illustrate the entire book pretty much as I wanted after full discussion of the content. It has been an extremely demanding but ultimately satisfying creative voyage, stretching over many months. Jeannine has also brought art back into the world of *Doctor Who*, which we should all celebrate. It's been a joy to work with her.

I would also like to thank Cam, the author, for his sterling work, for being a great guy to collaborate with, and for coming up with the cover concept while we sat on a bench on the grounds of Winchester Cathedral one sunny afternoon in May this past year. Oh, and his birthday is a day after mine! Scorpios both.

Finally, this book is dedicated to all the wonderful fan artists out there who post such varied and creative work purely for the love of it. You have been an inspiration.

—Andrew